NK
4370
.C87
WITHDRAWN

CONNOISSEUR'S LIBRARY

PORCELAIN

JOHN CUSHION

WORLD PUBLISHING
TIMES MIRROR
NEW YORK

Contents

Designed and produced by Harriet Bridgeman Limited

Published by The World Publishing Company
First American edition
First printing—1973
Copyright © Istituto Geografico De Agostini, Novara 1973
English edition © Orbis Publishing Limited, London 1973
All rights reserved
ISBN 0-529-05014-5
Library of Congress catalog card number: 72-10448
Phototypeset in England by Petty and Sons Limited, Leeds
Printed in Italy by IGDA, Novara

Library of Congress cataloging in publication data

Cushion, John Patrick.
Porcelain.

(Connoisseur's library)
Bibliography: p.
1. Porcelain. I. Title. II. Series:
Connoisseur's library (New York)
NK4370.C87 738.2 72-10448
ISBN 0-529-05014-5

WORLD PUBLISHING
TIMES MIRROR

Pottery and porcelain are among the most popular wares today in the field of antiques. The history of pottery is, of course, much older than that of porcelain – the clays used to produce earthenware can be found in almost every area of the world and the material does not require the high firing necessary for the production of porcelain. Porcelain can usually be recognized by its translucency, providing it has not been too heavily 'thrown' or cast, or fired at too low a temperature. The newcomer to the world of ceramics usually has difficulty however, in recognizing whether a piece is 'true' or 'hard-paste' porcelain, or 'soft-paste'.

The Chinese discovered the use of china-clay (*kaolin*) as early as the Han dynasty (BC 206–220 AD), but it was not until about 850 AD, during the T'ang dynasty that they discovered the second essential material, china-stone (*petuntse*). These two materials, when fired in a kiln to a temperature of about 1,350°C, fuse together to form a white and partially translucent mass. The Chinese described these two materials as the flesh and the skeleton of porcelain, the particles of the china-clay forming the frame for the flesh of the china-stone. The glaze of true porcelain is made from the china-stone, and can be fired at the same time as the body, hence, it 'fits' well and rarely gathers in tears or pools and hardly ever 'crazes' (the term used to describe the minute crackle of the glaze). Modelling and details remain crisp and clear and the enamel colours, when fired to the surface of the glaze, tend to remain on the surface in a bright and clear fashion. Chips or breakages invariably show the body to be a vitrified mass, with a distinct glassy sheen.

The Chinese porcelain was almost always made of this material and only a few unimportant late eighteenth-century wares are of a so-called 'soapstone' porcelain, similar to those made at Worcester and Caughley in England.

An early form of soft-paste porcelain, known as Medici porcelain, was first made in Italy, at Florence, from 1575 to 1587, but it was the French who first produced soft-paste in commercial quantities during the late seventeenth century at Saint-Cloud. Soft-paste is composed basically of white-firing clays, with varying amounts of 'frit' (equivalent to ground-up glass); the glaze actually consists of a thin layer of lead-glass. Generally the body of soft-paste porcelain did not lend itself to any fine detail of modelling; also the glaze was rather thicker and tended to clog up any fine features and also to craze. The colours on soft-paste usually tended to be partially absorbed by the glaze, giving a pleasingly soft effect. When chipped or broken, it will be seen to have a 'sugary' fracture.

Chinese porcelain

During the Sung dynasty (960–1279 AD) the finest porcelains made in China were the Ting wares of Ting Chou in Hopei province, in the north-east of China; the Lung-ch'uan and *ch'ing-pai*. The finest Ting wares were decorated with delicately incised patterns of flowers and foliage, emphasized by an ivory-tinted glaze. To the student, Lung-ch'uan and *ch'ing-pai* wares look somewhat similar. The former is the name of the place in the western part of the province of Chekiang where the near-white hard-paste porcelain was made. When decoration was used, it again consisted of either shallowly incised and usually sparse patterns or rather more crowded moulded decoration all under a bluish-green translucent celadon glaze. There are also some particularly fine examples decorated with full relief dragons. The glaze on the *ch'ing-pai* porcelain is more of a pale icy-blue tone. These latter wares were made in the Kiangsi province, which became the centre of the vast porcelain industry of China.

In 1279 the Sung dynasty was overthrown by the Mongols and porcelain fashions changed. During the Ming dynasty (1368–1644), the preference was obviously for painted decoration rather than form. From at least the middle of the fourteenth century great success was achieved with underglaze blue, a colour derived from the metallic oxide of cobalt. This colour was painted directly on to the body of the ware prior to the glazing, enabling such pieces to be completed in a single kiln-firing. These early blue designs were imitated a good deal in the earthenwares made in Persia, where true porcelain was never produced.

From the reign of the Emperor Ch'êng Hua (1465–87), the Chinese potter began to decorate his fine porcelain with enamel colours. The process consists of fusing the enamels (coloured glass) to the surface of the glaze at a temperature not exceeding about 800°C. If fired higher, these low-temperature colours start to burn away.

It was during the long reign of the Emperor K'ang Hsi

24701

Left: *Storage jar from the Yuan dynasty (1280–1368) (Christie, Manson and Woods, London).* Right: *Cache-pot from the St Cloud factory, near Paris (Victoria and Albert Museum, London)*

(1662–1722) that the porcelain centre of Ching-tê-chên reached its peak of production. Apart from the fine porcelains made for the use of the court, an enormous number of lower quality wares were made for export to Europe and the Near East. Chinese porcelain was in great demand by the various courts of Europe as, apart from silver, there was no alternative to the hard-paste porcelain of China.

The majority of the books written during the nineteenth century on the study of Chinese porcelains were written in France, hence many names given to various types of decoration are still referred to in the original French. It was during the reign of K'ang Hsi that the polychrome enamel palette of the *famille verte* became particularly popular throughout Europe. The decoration usually consisted of prolific flower and foliage patterns with birds or figures set in landscapes. The best painting had an apparently careless style and was totally different from the painstaking brushwork of a copyist.

Other '*familles*' were the *famille noire*, where the entire background to the decoration was painted in blackish brown, overpainted with a translucent green; and it was probably from the last years of the reign of K'ang Hsi that use was made of the rose-coloured enamel in *famille rose*. This colour was derived from chloride of gold and was first used in the late seventeenth century by European enamellers. The tones ranged from a pale pink to a deep crimson, depending on the amount of white used. The best *famille rose* was produced during the reign of the Emperor Yung Chêng (1723–35) when the decoration was sparse and in the best of taste. In the following reign of Ch'ien Lung (1736–95), the ground tended to be over-decorated.

From the middle of the seventeenth century many wares were transported to Europe by the ships of the various East India companies. These porcelains had often been decorated to order with the coat of arms or monogram of the customer. French prints and drawings were a further source of inspiration for decoration. Most of the enamel decoration was added to the porcelain at Canton, where all the actual trading was carried on. The Chinese decorators had great difficulty in painting European faces and in consequence all the characters appear with Oriental features, regardless of their nationality.

From the start of the Ming dynasty, wares were often painted in underglaze blue with the reign-mark of an Emperor; these marks are not always a true indication of period, and were often back-dated several reigns or even a dynasty. Initially, this practice was employed as a sign of veneration and not intended to deceive in the way that marks on nineteenth-century wares were sometimes deliberately back-dated.

Japanese porcelain

True porcelain was made in Japan from early in the seventeenth century, after deposits of the necessary materials had been discovered in Hizen. The neighbouring area of Arita was soon to become the centre of the porcelain industry of Japan; not Imari, which is a name so often wrongly used. Imari is simply the port from which the Japanese wares were shipped.

It was during the internal strife in China in the middle of the seventeenth century that the Dutch began to import large quantities of porcelain, decorated in a purple-toned underglaze blue. The later wares, which were to become even more popular in Europe, were the large red, blue and gilt dishes and garnitures of vases painted with a mass of flowers, including chrysanthemums, and motifs including scrolls and panels. Among the most beautiful of all Japanese porcelains were the Arita wares decorated in the so-called Kakiemon style, named after the Japanese potter Sakaida Kakiemon who is credited with introducing the pleasing designs of, 'The Hob-in-the-Well', 'Lady in the Pavilion', 'The Tiger and the Bamboo' and many others, all in soft reds, greenish-blues, turquoise, yellow and occasional underglaze blue.

A further well-known type of decoration was used on the

porcelains made from about 1660 at Kutani (the nine valleys), in the province of Kaga. Here the painting was bold and seemingly careless, the colours used being blue, dull yellow, rich purple, a dark, opaque red and a strong green. Many Kutani wares, especially those made during the nineteenth century, were completely covered with enamelling, leaving little trace of the coarse and heavy porcelain.

The term 'Nabeshima' originates from a prince of that name who established a porcelain factory at Okawachi in the neighbourhood of Arita in about 1660. Nabeshima wares were usually decorated with flowers and foliage and painted in soft underglaze blue under a smooth, flawless glaze, with pale enamel colours. Their typical style of painting was often so precise in manner as to be rather dull. In the same area, a further well-known class of porcelain was made for the princess of Hirado from about 1712. The decoration, on a flawless white porcelain body, was usually of figure subjects in landscapes painted in a violet-toned blue.

To-day the collector is more conversant with the comparatively common Satsuma ware, made at Satsuma on the island of Kyushu, which has been made in vast quantities for the European market since about 1860, and can only rarely be dated earlier. It includes cream-coloured wares painted with enamel colours and gilding and is usually very elaborately decorated.

From about 850 AD until about 1710 the only true porcelain manufactured throughout the entire world was that made in the Far East. There is little doubt that the first European country to become acquainted with this material was Italy; even Marco Polo, returning from his travels at the end of the thirteenth century, brought back samples of this rare and precious porcelain. It is, therefore, not surprising to learn that it was in Italy that the earliest European experiments were made to imitate this ware.

From 1575 until about 1587 the limited production of soft-paste porcelain took place in Florence at the instigation of the Grand Duke Francesco I de'Medici. This imitation porcelain was produced by combining eighty per cent of a white firing clay with twenty per cent of the ingredients of glass (frit); the decoration was in underglaze blue with an occasional purple outline in manganese oxide. There are only about sixty pieces of Medici porcelain known to be in existence to-day, nearly all in major museums.

Early French porcelain

The next serious attempt to produce porcelain in Europe was, to the best of our knowledge, made in France. There certainly seems enough evidence to support the allegation that from about 1673 Louis Poterat produced a certain amount of soft-paste porcelain at Rouen. The few pieces attributed to Poterat are of slightly bluish-green porcelain under a clear, wet-looking glaze. The underglaze blue decoration is very similar to the pendant-ornaments (lambrequin) that can be seen on Rouen tin-glazed earthenware (faience).

The porcelain made at Saint-Cloud, near Paris, by the

Glazed white porcelain figure from the Du Paquier factory (Victoria and Albert Museum, London)

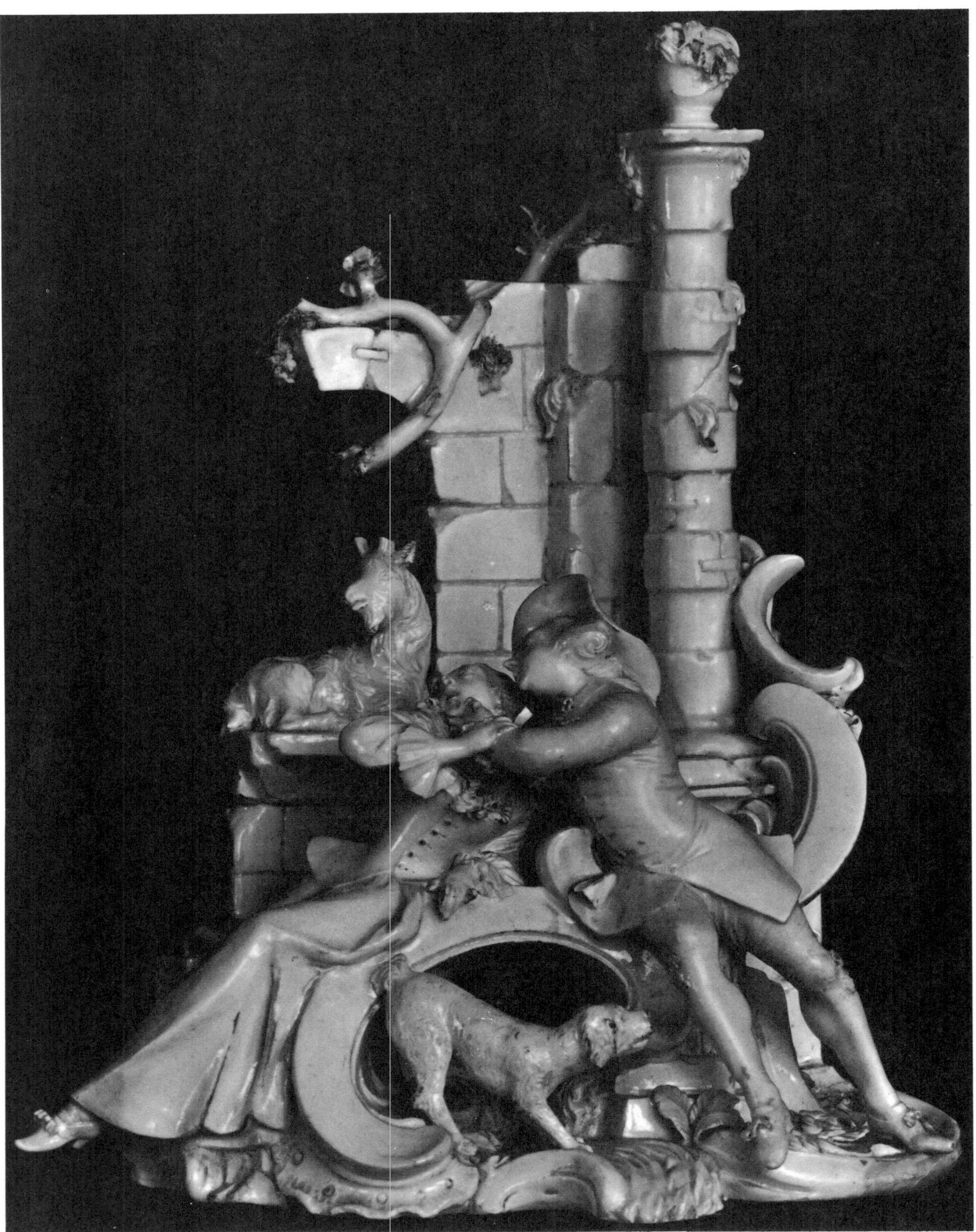

family of Pierre Chicaneau is better documented. Pierre Chicaneau, who also made faience, had seemingly produced a soft-paste porcelain prior to his death in 1678. His widow and family continued to improve upon his early productions until, by 1693, they were claiming that their wares equalled those of China.

Saint-Cloud soft-paste porcelain has much in common with the earliest wares made at the Chelsea factory in England. Their pieces were usually small, probably due to the difficulty of preventing them from warping in the firing, they were also heavily potted. Tablewares were often moulded to imitate artichokes; they also favoured square-sectioned handles and saucers with a raised ring to secure the cup. This was probably the earliest use of the *trembleuse* saucer. The porcelain of Saint-Cloud was in great demand by the Paris merchants (*marchands-merciers*) who often had pieces mounted with fine ormolu or silver. The factory finally closed in 1766.

The majority of the early European porcelain factories enjoyed the advantages of a wealthy patron. In the case of the factory established in 1725 at Chantilly, it was the Prince de Condé. The Prince had a very fine collection of Japanese hard-paste porcelain decorated in the Kakiemon style and so some of the finest early porcelain made at Chantilly was decorated in this same Japanese manner. In order to make the creamy soft-paste porcelain of Chantilly look more like the white hard-paste body of Japanese porcelain, the glaze was made completely white and opaque with tin oxide (as used on tin-glazed earthenware). During this period (1725 to about 1740), the mark used was a French hunting-horn in red enamel. During the second half of the eighteenth century, Far Eastern styles gave way to more original, but duller decoration, often consisting of sprays of flowers in either underglaze blue or blue enamel. This so-called 'Chantilly sprig' was imitated and sometimes confused with similar decoration on the soft-paste porcelain made at the English factory of Caughley in Shropshire in about 1780.

Although the original Chantilly factory closed in about 1800, other concerns in the same area continued to make similar wares marked with the same hunting-horn, which was sometimes accompanied by the initials of the proprietor, such as 'P' for Pigory, or 'M.A.' for Michel-Isaac Aaron.

Among the most beautiful soft-paste porcelains ever made were those produced at Mennecy from about 1734. These wares were at times marked with the incised initials 'D.V.', for the patron, the Duc de Villeroy. The flower-painting in a palette of rose-pinks, bright blues and brownish-greens, seems to illustrate the sinking of the colours into a soft-paste porcelain glaze, producing a more attractive effect than that on any other factory's wares. The rare figures produced at Mennecy were equally charming and were obviously inspired in many instances by the chubby children painted by François Boucher. These groups usually took the form of centrepieces, with the children precariously balanced on a pile of rocks and seemingly in danger of falling off.

Group from the Nymphenburg factory by F. A. Bustelli, c.1760. Marked with a shield with the arms of Bavaria (Victoria and Albert Museum, London)

German and Austrian porcelain

When Augustus II, King of Poland, succeeded to the title of Elector of Saxony in 1694, one of the first demands he made of his economic advisor, Ehrenfried Walther von Tschirnhaus, was for an efficient survey of the mineral wealth of Saxony. One of the aims of this undertaking was to locate the ingredients that were essential for the manufacture of the porcelain that was being produced by the Far Eastern potters.

From about 1704 Tschirnhaus was assisted by a young alchemist, J. F. Böttger, who had previously rashly claimed to be able to produce gold from base metals. Their first experiments resulted in the manufacture of a fine red stoneware, similar to but much harder and more finely grained, than that being made at the same time at Yi-hsing in China, Delft in the Netherlands and Staffordshire in England.

The first white porcelain produced at Meissen, in 1708, contained alabaster as an alternative to china-stone, resulting in a rather drably coloured body. It was probably almost 1720 before china-stone and china-clay were used together to produce an even whiter and more highly fired (1,400°C) porcelain than that of the Orient.

Tschirnhaus died in 1708, and so most of the credit for the establishment of the 'red and white porcelain' manufactory in 1710, goes to Böttger. The production took place in the Albrechtsberg fortress at Meissen, twelve miles north west of Dresden. It is essential that today's collectors are specific over whether a piece of porcelain was made at the actual Meissen factory, which is still in production, or in another factory, possibly one of the less important Dresden factories set up in the city itself from about the middle of the nineteenth century. Meissen adopted the famous 'crossed swords' as a factory-mark in about 1723; the later Dresden concerns often introduced somewhat similar and confusing marks. The Meissen swords should always be in underglaze blue, with the rare exception of the blue enamel version sometimes used on wares decorated in imitation of the Japanese Kakiemon style.

The decoration on the early wares consisted mainly of gilding or purple lustre, the few enamel colours used being generally of rather poor quality. It was in 1720 that Stölzel, the renegade Meissen kiln-master, returned from Vienna with the brilliant young enamel-painter J. G. Höroldt. This painter not only produced the many copies of Oriental wares so sought after by the Elector of Saxony but also introduced beautifully painted *chinoiserie* styles of his own invention.

The first porcelain modeller to be appointed to the factory was a young Dresden sculptor, J. G. Kirchner, who was engaged primarily from 1727–28 and from 1730–33 in the modelling of large animals and vases until he was succeeded by the more famous modeller J. J. Kändler, who worked at the factory from 1731.

In 1733 Augustus the Strong was succeeded by his son Augustus III, who preferred fine paintings to porcelain, and so the running of the factory was entrusted to his chief minister, Count Heinrich Von Brühl. Kändler was

Two cups and a plate from the Vezzi factory (Museo Civico, Turin)

requested to turn his attention to designing tablewares decorated with high relief and figure modelling. Among the more famous services produced was that made for Count Brühl himself, the renowned Swan Service, which comprised about 2,200 pieces, all decorated with either reliefs, or fully modelled swans, marine deities, mermaids, shells and other such related subjects. Kändler is, however, probably better known for his series of small figures in porcelain, modelled after the characters which featured in the traditional theatre of the Italian Comedy.

Meissen can be regarded as the fashion-setter for European porcelain up until about 1760 when Saxony was at war with Prussia and the factory was occupied by the troops of Frederick the Great. The factory continues to this day, but their productions never again matched the early wares.

Claudius Innocentius Du Paquier had endeavoured to produce hard-paste porcelain in Vienna from 1717, but it was not until he persuaded Samuel Stölzel, the kiln-master from Meissen, to join him, that he was successful in producing a true porcelain. His earliest wares often had a bluish-grey body under a slightly smoky-coloured glaze.

Du Paquier's factory became state owned in 1744, when the factory-mark of a shield with bars was adopted. From 1784 the factory was under the management of Sorgenthal, and finally closed in 1866. The porcelains made in the Du Paquier period consisted mainly of fine tableware of extreme baroque forms, decorated with enamel scroll-work, shell-like palmettes and intricate lattice-like gilding. These showed a great deal of originality. During the State Period their wares were more often fashioned after those of Meissen, especially the figures of shepherds, vendors, waiters and musicians. From the late eighteenth century, Vienna endeavoured to recapture the forms of classical antiquity, often showing a tendency to over-decorate with lavish enamelling and gilding.

For many years Meissen enjoyed almost sole monopoly of hard-paste manufacture in Europe, but towards the middle of the eighteenth century it became increasingly difficult to keep safe the many secrets involved in its production, and many rival factories started the manufacture of good quality useful wares and figures, often with the assistance of renegade Meissen workers.

The porcelain produced at Höchst-am-Main from about 1750 was at first a rather coarse material with a milky-white glaze. Their tablewares were often decorated with landscapes, *chinoiseries* or flower-painting in the Meissen manner, but coupled with elaborate rococo scroll-work frames picked out in deep purple or lavish gilding. The early work of the modeller Simon Feilner is very much in the bold baroque manner of Kändler and this is particularly noticeable on his figures from the Italian Comedy and his peasant characters.

The factory closed in 1796, and their moulds passed into the hands of factories at Damm and Bonn, who made poor quality tin-glazed earthenware reproductions of the earlier models. In the early years of this century the moulds were again used by a firm at Passau, who made the same models in a hard-paste porcelain. These later reproductions are invariably marked with the six-spoked wheel, the original factory-mark.

The original Nymphenburg factory was established at Neudeck, near Munich, in about 1747, but it was not until 1753 that a fine quality hard-paste porcelain was produced with the aid of the nomadic arcanist J. J. Ringler.

The man whose name is particularly associated with Nymphenburg is that of the modeller Franz Anton Bustelli, and whilst Kändler must be acknowledged as the outstanding modeller in the baroque style, there is little doubt that Bustelli was the master during the succeeding fashion for rococo. His treatment of this wave-like, restless movement was outstanding; his individual figures particularly reflect it, the best examples being his fine figures of the Italian Comedy characters.

The Nymphenburg factory was moved to a building adjacent to the Palace of Nymphenburg in 1761, where it continued to enjoy the patronage of Prince Max III Joseph of Bavaria. Since 1862 production has continued under a private company and many of their wares are still being made after the original eighteenth-century models. The early mark was an impressed diapered shield.

Hard-paste porcelain was first produced in Frankenthal by Paul Hannong of Strasbourg in 1755, the factory being purchased by the Elector Carl Theodor in 1762. Useful wares and figures of a very high quality continued to be produced until the closure of the concern in 1800. The rococo style of decoration on Frankenthal porcelain is probably the most extravagant to be seen on any porcelain. As with so many contemporary factories, there was a greater individuality of treatment on the figure-subjects than on the tablewares. The early figures and groups produced by W. Lanz tend to be on a smaller scale than the average contemporary pieces and often show theatrical poses on grass-covered bases edged with gilt rococo scroll-work.

The figures of the brothers Lück had a more healthy and robust appearance with highly elaborate rococo bases often pierced in the late Derby fashion. The later modellers A. Bauer and J. P. Melchior produced figures of a classical nature, but sometimes a little too voluptuous to suggest their antique origins.

Later Italian porcelain

The first hard-paste porcelain factory to be established in Venice was that of Francesco Vezzi (1651–1740). This concern was active from 1720–27, during which time its porcelain body usually equalled that of Meissen in quality. Teapots of either globular or octagonal form were particularly popular, the enamel decoration often consisting of homely-looking characters in fancy dress. Vezzi also produced some very attractive cups, made in imitation of Chinese *blanc-de-chine*, with applied prunus designs.

The later Venetian factory of Cozzi produced tablewares and a few figures, these being in a rather inferior grey body with an ill-fitting, wet-looking glaze. The Italian

Teapot from the Vincennes factory (Victoria and Albert Museum, London)

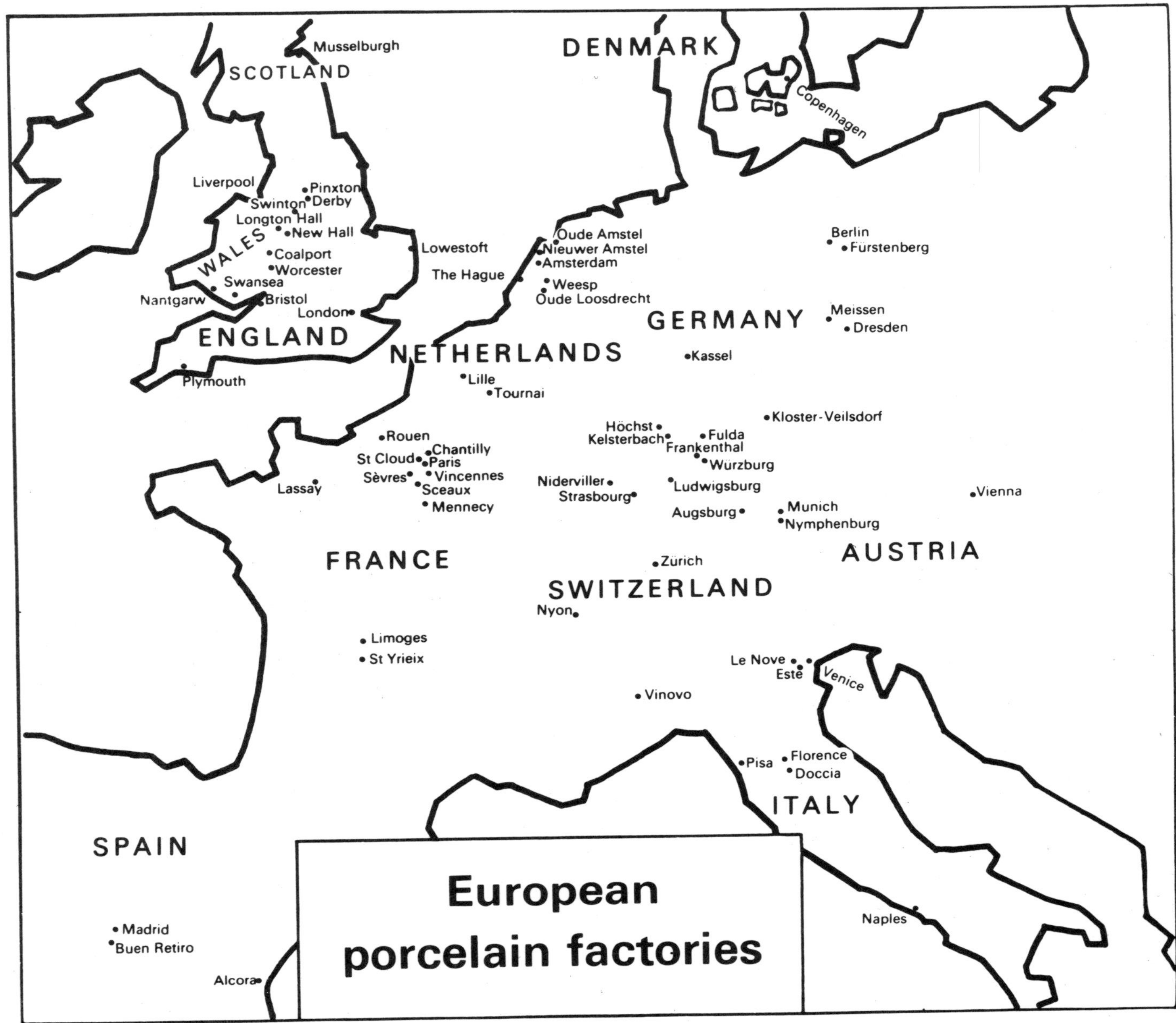

porcelain modellers never really understood the rococo style; their approach was invariably too fussy and they were more at ease with the later neoclassical fashions. The factory enjoyed many privileges and subsidies, enabling it to continue in production from 1764 until the final occupation of the factory by foreign troops in 1812.

A further long-established Italian porcelain factory is that founded in 1735 at Doccia, near Florence, by Carlo Ginori. This factory continues to this day under the name of Richard-Ginori. Their early paste was hard and grey in comparison with the contemporary Meissen. Teapots with baroque snake-spouts and high-domed lids are very typical of their early wares where overfiring often resulted in the glaze taking on the 'orange-peel' texture normally associated with salt-glazed stoneware. This high firing also often resulted in the underglaze blue taking on a greyish-black tone.

Between about 1770 and 1790, the grey body was often disguised by the use of a glaze made both white and opaque by the addition of tin oxide, a type of glaze normally used only on earthenwares. It was at Doccia that the original 'figure subjects in low relief' were produced. These usually depicted Bacchanalian or hunting scenes, a style often copied on late nineteenth-century German wares, fraudulently marked with a crowned 'N'. This mark, if correct, is found only on the soft-paste porcelain of the Royal Naples factory founded in 1771.

The most beautiful porcelain ever produced in Italy was at the Capodimonte factory, established near Naples by Charles of Bourbon in 1743 and continuing there until being transferred to Buen Retiro near Madrid in 1759, where production continued until 1800. The mark used at both places is always the *fleur-de-lis*, impressed, in blue or gilt, never a crowned 'N'.

The beauty of Capodimonte porcelain is best seen on the many figures designed by Gricc, who is recognized as one of the most versatile modellers. Lovers, Italian Comedy characters and fisherfolk, together with religious subjects, feature in the great variety of models attributed to him. The outstanding feature of Gricc's figures are their very small heads with eyes painted with stripes and dots.

French porcelain

The porcelains of Vincennes and Sèvres are numbered among the most priceless of all ceramic treasures. The concern was started as early as 1738 in a royal château at Vincennes, moving to a new building at Sèvres in 1756. Despite the early start it was nearly 1749 before good quality wares were produced in any quantity, but due to the high costs of production the factory would have closed in 1759 if Madame de Pompadour had not persuaded Louis XV to purchase the factory himself.

The early soft-paste wares were in the graceful French shapes of the period, entirely divorced from those of Meissen; jugs with long, cylindrical necks, ice-pails, *cache-pots*, *pot-pourri* vases, and slender vases with trumpet-shaped mouths, usually decorated with French versions of Meissen flowers or Watteau-like scenes.

The history of the Vincennes and Sèvres factories is well documented; it is known when the beautiful coloured grounds were introduced and the names and devices or initials of the majority of the painters and gilders are recorded and published in several different books. We know what type of decoration the painters specialized in, and when they were employed at the factory. In about 1750 the crossed Ls cipher of Louis was first adopted as a factory-mark, and from 1753 the letters of the alphabet were used within the double Ls' to denote the year of production, 'A' for 1753, 'AA' for 1778 ending with 'PP' in 1793, the time when the concern was taken over by the Republic, after which the 'R.F.' (*République Française*) replaced the royal device.

The earliest ground-colour appears to have been the fine *'bleu lapis'* (an underglaze blue), which usually has an attractive variation in depth of colour. The turquoise (*bleu céleste*) was used from 1752, the rare yellow (*jaune jonquille*) followed in 1753, pea green in 1756, and the powdery pink of *rose* (not *rose Pompadour*) in 1757. The authenticity of a piece of Vincennes or Sèvres porcelain can often be judged by the quality of the gilding alone, which was outstanding.

In 1768 the materials necessary for the production of true porcelain were discovered at Saint-Yrieix, near Limoges, and from about 1770–72 soft-paste porcelain gradually gave way to the cheaper and more practical material of true porcelain. Soft-paste was finally abandoned in about 1804.

The French were seemingly the first to leave their porcelain figures, in the unglazed and undecorated state known as 'biscuit', and as early as 1753 Lazare Duvaux, one of the best known of the Paris *marchands-merciers*, was advertizing the sale of such figures. The best-known modeller of these biscuit figures was Etienne-Maurice Falconet, who was employed at the factory from 1756–65, after which he moved to St. Petersburg in Russia.

The new collector will often be confused by the many pieces of porcelain which bear the marks of Sèvres but have rather inferior decoration on what is obviously a piece of early soft-paste. These are wares which have been redecorated in the early years of the nineteenth century in the more expensive and sought-after styles; the ground colours are usually uneven and pitted, the date-letter often pre-dates the style of decoration. The firm of Samson of Paris made many copies of Sèvres biscuit figures but their mark usually took the form of four interlaced Ss rather than the correctly crossed Ls.

Figure of the actor Henry Woodward from the Bow Factory, c.1750 (Victoria and Albert Museum, London)

Russian porcelain

As early as 1718, the Russians were endeavouring to learn the secret of the manufacture of true porcelain; they even sent an agent to Meissen, but he was unsuccessful. Their next attempt involved the impostor Conrad Hunger from Meissen, but he too proved to be an expensive failure.

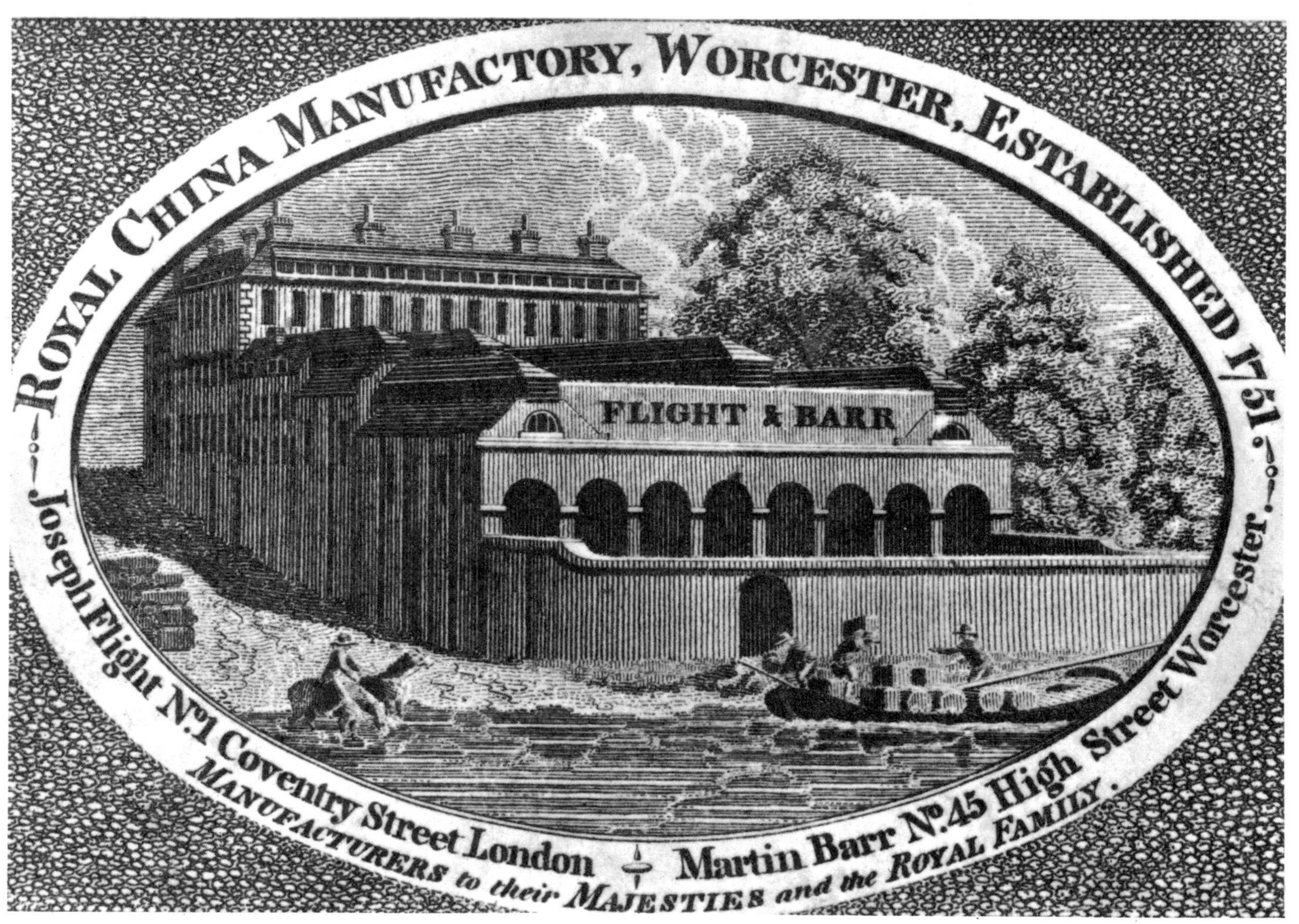

Trade-card for the Worcester factory, designed by J. Ross c.1801 in the Flight and Barr period

The first successful hard-paste porcelain was not made in Russia until about 1750 when Dmitri Vinogradov was in charge of the Imperial Porcelain factory at St. Petersburg. His productions were mostly after Chinese or Meissen models, but actually in simpler styles. The factory flourished and by 1756 was employing seventy workers. By the time Catherine II came to the throne in 1762, the factory was capable of producing wares to equal those of any other European factory.

The most successful independent manufacturer was Francis Gardner who was granted permission by the Department of Manufacturers to establish his factory at the village of Verbilki, near Moscow, in 1766. The Gardner factory was patronized by Catherine and some very ornate services were produced to her orders, usually decorated with various insignia of Imperial Orders of Chivalry. Gardner porcelain is today particularly associated with the delightful biscuit porcelain figures covered with matt enamels which depict a whole variety of traders and peasants. The factory continued until 1892 when it was taken over by the firm of Kuznetsov.

Other minor Russian factories were established in about 1780 but most of these concerns were forced to close at the time of the Napoleonic invasion of 1812.

English porcelain

To the best of our knowledge no porcelain was made in England prior to about 1745. It was at this time that the Flemish silversmith Nicholas Sprimont (d.1771), is considered to have started to manufacture a glassy, soft-paste porcelain at Chelsea, in London. He was probably aided initially by a jeweller, Charles Gouyn, who was also from the Continent.

Chelsea porcelain can be divided into five distinct periods, four of which are named by the type of mark sometimes used during those years. Thus the first period (1745–*c.*1749) is known as the 'incised triangle' period; during these years the body was made of a glassy, soft paste with a good, clear glaze which only rarely crazed. These early wares consisted mainly of small jugs, salts, sauce-boats and teapots, often in the form of silver-shapes that Sprimont had previously made in metal.

During the second period (*c.*1749–52) the mark used was a small applied oval medallion with an anchor in relief – the 'raised anchor' period. From this time there was a distinct improvement in the quality of the porcelain which was now also suitable for the production of figures. It was during the 'raised anchor' period and the subsequent 'red anchor' period (*c.*1752–*c.*1758) that Chelsea wares began to look distinctly whiter; this was due to the use of a small quantity of tin oxide, the ingredient normally used to render the glaze on earthenwares opaque.

It was during the 'raised anchor' and 'red anchor' periods that the Chelsea workers imitated so many Meissen wares and figures direct from the original pieces which were put at their disposal by the British Ambassador at the court of Dresden, Sir Charles Hanbury Williams. Many of these tablewares were made in such naturalistic forms as rabbits, chickens, lettuces, cauliflowers and fish.

The last independent period of the Chelsea factory was from about 1758–70, the 'gold anchor' period, during which time the mark consisted of a small gold anchor. This mark is still imitated today, usually on poor quality hard-paste figures, most probably of German origin. It was during this period that Chelsea made so many tablewares and vases after the rococo fashions popularized by the Sèvres factory of France.

In 1770 the Chelsea factory was taken over by William Duesbury, already proprietor of the Derby factory. Both factories were run by Duesbury until 1784, when the Chelsea factory was finally closed. It was during this so-called 'Chelsea-Derby' period that so many good and practical tablewares were made, often in neoclassical styles. The mark was a gold anchor together with a gold 'D' (for either Derby or Duesbury) either in monogram form or side by side.

Recent excavations have proved that the site of the Bow porcelain factory was actually on the Essex side of the River Lea, and not within the boundaries of London. Although a patent was taken out in 1744, this was for the production of the necessary materials for the making of porcelain. It was probably not until 1747 that soft-paste porcelain was made at the Bow factory in any commercial quantities.

Bow appears to have been the first English factory to produce a soft-paste porcelain containing calcined animal bone which enabled the Bow factory to produce a much stronger body than the earlier Chelsea factory. At the peak of their production over three hundred workers were engaged, mainly in the production of tablewares decorated with underglaze blue in the Chinese fashion.

Chelsea figures and some of their hollow-wares were made by the 'slip-casting' process whereby watered-down clay was poured into hollow plaster of Paris moulds. At Bow the rather clumsier method of press-moulding was used, the dough-like clay being pressed into the walls of the mould by hand. From about 1762 Bow wares were often painted with a red enamel factory-mark consisting of a small anchor and a dagger.

The factory was taken over, and closed, by William Duesbury of the Derby works in 1776.

It was in 1757 that Robert Browne and three partners established a soft-paste porcelain factory at Lowestoft in East Anglia, a concern which continued in production until about 1799. Their wares were only decorated in underglaze-blue up until about 1770 after which enamel colours were also used.

The porcelains made at Lowestoft consisted mainly of modest tablewares and small decorative vases, often decorated in the *chinoiserie* style. Certain constantly recurring features aid identification; the saucers nearly always have three small regularly spaced blemishes in the glaze on the extreme rim, caused by the Lowestoft method of supporting the wares on stilts during the glazing stage; small blue strokes were often painted alongside the joints of the handles to the main bodies and many of their handles have a slightly protruding section at the lower joint, referred to as a 'kick'.

The term 'Chinese Lowestoft' is completely erroneous and there is no relation whatsoever between the hard-paste export porcelain of China and the charming soft-paste wares of the English factory of Lowestoft.

Some of the most beautiful porcelain figures made at Derby were the work of André Planché, a potter who had apparently learnt the secret constituents of a fine quality soft-paste porcelain on the Continent. These wares, made from about 1750–56, were sometimes decorated by William Duesbury who at that time was a decorator of pottery and porcelain made at several different factories.

It was in 1756 that William Duesbury became the proprietor of the Derby factory, where he endeavoured to make his wares and figures look more like those of Meissen by colouring the glaze with cobalt. These wares were often decorated with the so-called 'dishevelled birds', moths, or flowers with thread-like stems, and often included a colour referred to as 'dirty turquoise'.

It was not until about 1782 that Derby figures and table-wares were marked with a crown, crossed-batons and 'D'. This mark was painted in blue or purple enamel until about 1800 after which it was usually in red; on some figures the mark was incised.

Some of the most beautiful landscape painting to be found on English porcelain were scenes of famous beauty spots in the Derbyshire countryside, painted at the Derby factory by Zachariah Boreman. The factory was run by Robert Bloor from about 1812 and finally closed in 1848. The present-day firm of Royal Crown Derby Porcelain Limited was not established until 1876.

In 1748 a porcelain factory was established in Bristol by Lund and Miller. Their porcelain was a soft-paste but contained soapstone (steatite) which made a fine quality porcelain, advertized as having been tested with boiling water. There seems little doubt that the 1751 partnership of the Worcester factory was formed in order to take over this factory, an intention they achieved in 1752. Recent excavations on the original Worcester site have proved that it is very difficult to separate the unmarked Bristol wares from those made in the early years at Worcester.

Apart from a small number of rather poor quality figures made in about 1770, Worcester concentrated on the production of good quality tablewares, the majority of which were decorated in underglaze blue. It was not until about 1765 that they started to make many more colourful wares in the style of the 'gold anchor' period at Chelsea.

The early years of Worcester, from 1751–76, are referred to by collectors as the 'Dr. Wall' period. After the death of Dr. Wall the factory continued under Davis, the chemist of the concern, until taken over by Flight in 1783. This period is now called the 'Davis and Flight' period and covers the years 1776–93. Other partnerships ran the factory until 1862 when the present-day Worcester Royal Porcelain Company Limited was formed.

In about 1772 Thomas Turner, who had acquired his knowledge concerning the manufacture of soapstone porcelain at Worcester, left that factory to start his own manufactory at Caughley (pronounced 'Calfley') in Shropshire. Until recently there was a good deal of confusion over the blue-printed wares made at these two factories, but excavations on their sites have made identification of the pieces a great deal easier. For many years wares with a mark consisting of a number (1–9) disguised as a Chinese character were thought to be Caughley productions, but these marks are now known to indicate Worcester wares of about 1776–93. Further confusion arose in the past due to the fact that the engraver Robert Hancock also worked at both factories and consequently very similar patterns appear on their wares. The finding of 'wasters' on the factory sites have now enabled these designs to be attributed with more certainty.

The Worcester factory records have also proved that many pieces of Caughley porcelain were sent by Turner to the decorating establishment of Chamberlain at Worcester, where they were sometimes painted with exotic birds and flowers in enamel colours and decorated with lavish gilding.

The Caughley concern was taken over by John Rose of the Coalport factory in 1799 and he continued to produce wares at Caughley until about 1812. During this Caughley/Coalport period, Rose produced a certain amount of hard-paste porcelain, which was until recently often attributed to New Hall.

To the best of our knowledge, the only porcelain to have been made in Staffordshire during the middle of the eighteenth century was produced at the short-lived factory at Longton Hall, where a very glassy soft-paste porcelain was made from 1749–60. Despite the fact that these wares are often of poor quality, they are eagerly sought after by collectors. The Staffordshire earthenware potters seemingly found it difficult to adapt their skills to the more sophisticated material of porcelain.

The best-known name concerned with Longton Hall is William Littler, who probably learnt how to produce porcelain whilst working at one of the early London factories. Littler later set up a pottery at West Pans in Scotland where he produced wares and decorated early pieces of Longton Hall to special order.

True porcelain was not produced in Britain until 1768 when William Cookworthy, a chemist, established a factory at Plymouth. The concern was transferred to Bristol in 1770 where production continued until 1781, when the remaining years of the patent concerning the exclusive use of china-clay and china-stone for the manufacture of porcelain were sold to a group of Staffordshire potters who formed the New Hall Company.

The earliest wares made at Plymouth were often defective, due to the workers' limited experience of firing wares at such high temperatures. The underglaze blue decoration often fired to a greyish-black tone, fire-cracks often occurred and the glaze was frequently stained by the smoke from the kiln. From about 1773, when Richard Champion took over as proprietor, the wares began to justify his claim that they coupled the hardness of Dresden (Meissen) with the elegance of Sèvres.

The hard-paste porcelain of New Hall was almost identical to that of Champion's at Bristol but the glaze was usually softer and more brilliant. In about 1812, New Hall, in common with many other Staffordshire factories, started to manufacture bone china, a very translucent, white body composed of the ingredients of true porcelain and fifty per cent calcined animal bone.

The name of William Billingsley (d.1828) is popularly associated with naturalistic flower painting and high-quality gilding. He worked at Derby, Pinxton, Mansfield, Worcester, Torksey and Wirksworth, sometimes with well-established factories and sometimes merely as an independent decorator. It was always Billingsley's ambition to become owner of his own porcelain factory, which he achieved in 1813 at Nantgarw in South Wales. Within the year, lack of capital had compelled him to move his undertaking to the Cambrian Pottery at Swansea where he stayed for about three years, after which he returned for a short while to Nantgarw. In 1819, Billingsley left to work for John Rose at Coalport, Shropshire.

The early porcelain of Nantgarw was in either the revived rococo style or the Empire style and, although beautiful, it was very difficult to fire successfully. Much of the porcelain produced at Nantgarw, Swansea and the later Coalport factory was enamelled in London for well-known retailers, but usually in a garish and somewhat overdecorated manner.

The factories of John Rose of Coalport, the Bramelds of Rockingham and Mintons, all produced very elaborately decorated wares from about 1825. Knowledge concerning these wares has, over the past few years, become available in more detail and it is now recognized that Coalport was certainly not the only factory to decorate their wares with the full-relief applied flowers; many such examples were also made by Mintons. Wares have also been wrongly attributed to the Yorkshire factory at Swinton, popularly known as Rockingham; there is for example, good reason to suppose that those little shaggy poodles and the pastille-burners in the form of cottages and castles were never made at this factory.

Thomas Minton started his factory at Stoke, in Staffordshire, in 1793 and to this day their wares have maintained a very high quality. Since the present management recently made their pattern-books available, it is often possible to attribute accurately unmarked wares to this pottery rather than simply to Staffordshire.

American porcelain

There seems little doubt that Andrew Duché, who was experimenting with porcelain clays at Savannah in Georgia from about 1740, had at least some success; but the true identification of his wares remains in doubt to this day.

It was in 1769 that Bonnin and Morris of Philadelphia were advertizing their 'New China Ware'. This porcelain, which has now been identified through wasters found on the site, is very similar to the soft-paste porcelain that was being made at a slightly earlier date at the Bow factory in England. The wares so far identified include shell centre-pieces, sauce-boats and fruit-bowls, all decorated in underglaze blue.

Philadelphia was also the city where William Ellis Tucker first produced a hard-paste porcelain for which he won an award in 1827. His tablewares, vases, jugs and pitchers were very similar to those being made in France at the same time.

PORCELAIN MARKS

RANCE

AINT CLOUD (Seine-et-Oise)
1670-
1678 - 1766
ft paste porcelain — incised

HANTILLY (Oise)
'25 - c. 1800 soft - paste porcelain
d enamel and occasionally black
r the early period, underglaze -
ue and occasionally crimson for
e later period

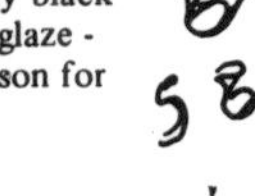

Chantilly

ENNECY - VILLEROY (Ile - de- France)
'34 - 1806
ft - paste porcelain and faience
otected by Louis - Francois de Neufville
734 - 1748 Paris
748 - 1773 Mennecy
773 - 1806 Bourg - la - Reine — D·V·

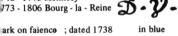

ark on faience ; dated 1738 — in blue

·D·V· ~DV~

rly wares in Japanese style — in red

iusual marks
the middle
id late period

D.V. in black — D·V· in blue — DV incised

EVRES (occasionally established at Vincennes
738 - present
oft and hard - paste porcelain
eigns of Louis XV and Louis XVI
about 1745 - 1793)

arks used before 1753 — in blue enamel

in underglaze blue — in blue enamel

ark with date - letter for 1753 — in blue enamel

ERMANY

EISSEN (nr. Dresden, Saxony)
ard paste porcelain
710 - present
ossed - swords mark
dopted 1724 — in blue or black enamel

arly examples of crossed swords
ark, 1724 - 1725

underglaze blue

725 - 1763 — underglaze blue

OCHST (nr. Mayence)
aience
746 - 1758
ounded by Adam Friedrich von Lowenfinck
actory marks with those of painters:
eorge Friedrich Hess
746 - 1750

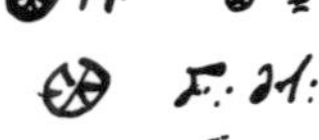

r his son Ignatz, c. 1750

robably mark of Simon Feilner
750 - 1753

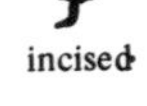

incised

NYMPHENBURG (nr. Munich Bavaria)
753 - present
ard - paste porcelain
Bustelli period '
754 - 1765

impressed

FRANKENTHAL (Palatine)
hard - paste porcelain
1755 - 1799

' Paul Hannong,' 1755 - 1756 and perhaps later (also on Strasburg porcelain 1753 - 1754) — PH impressed

' Paul Hannong Frankenthal,' 1755- 1756 possibly until 1759 — PH PHF impressed

AUSTRIA

VIENNA
Claudius Innocentius Du Paquier
1719- 1864
hard- paste porcelain
Du Paquier period (1719 - 1744)
mark on Chinese style c. 1720- 30 — in blue

ITALY

VENICE
18th century-
hard-paste porcelain

Vezzi factory, 1719-20 to 1727
c. 1720-27 — Venezia. incised in blue

DOCCIA (nr. Florence)
1735 - present
hard - paste porcelain
late 18th and first half of 19th century

all in blue red or gold

NAPLES
late 18th century

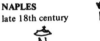

all impressed

incised or red — underglaze blue

CAPODIMONTE 1743 - 1759
soft - paste porcelain
King Charles III of Bourbon

impressed

on figures and groups
about 1745

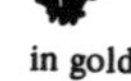

in gold

on useful wares and occasionally figures. Also used at Buen Retiro

RUSSIA

ST PETERSBURG (later Petrograd)
1744 -
hard - paste porcelain

impressed

Russian Imperial Porcelain Factory period of Elizabeth, 1741 - 1762

FRANCIS GARDNER
c. 1765-1891

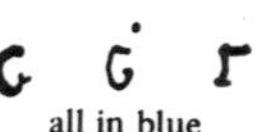

all in blue

ENGLAND

CHELSEA (London)

Chelsea

c.1745-1784 soft-paste porcelain
early mark of 'incised triangle'.
c. 1745-1750 — incised

' raised-anchor', c. 1749-52,
laterly picked out in red — in applied relief

' red-anchor',
1752-1756

painted in red
also found in underglaze blue, blue enamel, and purple enamel

c. 1758-1769

in gold

CHELSEA-DERBY period 1770-1784

red or gold — gold

BOW
on figures and other late pieces

in red — in underglaze blue & red

WILLIAM DUESBURY & CO'.,
c. 1760

incised

DERBY
1784-1810

blue, crimson or purple

' Duesbury & Kean',
c. 1795 — blue, crimson or purple

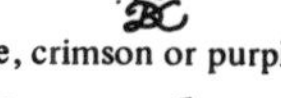

Bloor period,
1811-1848 — in red — printed in red

LOWESTOFT (Suffolk)
1757-1802
soft-paste porcelain

Allen
Lowestoft

Allen, Robert, b. 1744, d. 1835, decorator at Lowestoft factory and independent enameller from 1802

WORCESTER

factory marks 1755-1790:

underglaze blue — red — printed in blue

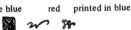

underglaze blue

mark on early
blue-printed wares

underglaze blue

on ' Japan patterns ',
c. 1760-1775 — underglaze blue

imitation of Meissen mark

underglaze blue

' Flight ' period,
1783-1792
(crown added 1788)

Flight — underglaze blue — Flight red or blue

' Flight and Barr 'period ,
1792-1807 — Flight & Barr in red

LONGTON HALL
(nr. Newcastle-under-Lyme)

c. 1750-1760
Littler, William
soft-paste porcelain — all in blue

BRISTOL
hard-paste porcelain

Coolworthy's and Champion's factory 1770-1781
early mark during Coolworthy's ownership (also used at Plymouth)

'BRISTOL' 'BRISTOLL' 'BRISTOLL 1750'
all impressed in relief

in underglaze blue, blue enamel, red or gold — in blue enamel

NANTGARW (Glamorgan)
1813-1822
William Billingsley and Samuel Walker — NANT-GARW C.W. impressed

'CW' stands for ' China Works ' (transfered to Swansea for a year or two from 1814; resumed before 1817)

SWANSEA (Glamorgan)
1765-1870
pottery and porcelain

SWANSEA
impressed or printed in red

porcelain marks,
1814-1822

SWANSEA impressed — SWANSEA in red Swansea in red — SWANSEA impressed

COALPORT
1830-1850

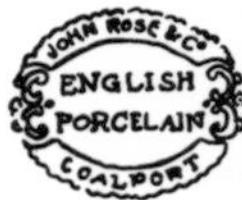

MINTON
1793-
Minton's Ltd.,
Thomas Minton and Herbert Minton (son)
general pottery
1822-1836 — in blue enamel

ROCKINGHAM
porcelain also produced from about 1825
1826-1842 crest of Earl Fitzwilliam, Marquis of Rockingham, a patron

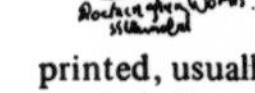

in relief — printed, usually in red

Glossary of terms

Biscuit. Fired but unglazed porcelain or, more rarely, pottery. Used in porcelain as a medium for modelling.
Bocage. Background of flowers and foliage used in figures or groups in the eighteenth and nineteenth centuries.
Celadon. Chinese porcelain wares with glazes of varying shades of light green and grey containing iron oxides.
China clay (kaolin) and **China stone (petuntse).** The two essential ingredients of hard-paste, or 'true' porcelain.
Crackle. Fine cracks in the glaze, deliberately caused, as a means of decoration.
Crazing. Fine cracks in the glaze, normally unintentional, as a result of the unequal shrinking of glaze and body.
Deutsche Blumen. The painting of flowers in a naturalistic style, first used on porcelain at the Meissen factory in about 1740.
Enamel colours. Colours, usually on a lead base, painted over the glaze and having a lower firing temperature than the glaze itself. These are termed '*petit feu*' colours.
Felspathic glaze. Glazes containing felspar rock. Used on porcelain and stonewares, and fired at a high temperature.
Frit. Used in the making of soft-paste porcelain; a partially fused composition of sand and fluxes equivalent to ground glass.
Glaze. Glassy coating on porcelain and pottery rendering them impervious to liquids.
Hard paste. 'True' porcelain. Made for centuries by the Chinese, the ingredients remained secret in Europe until discovered in 1708 by J. F. Böttger of the Meissen factory.
Lustre. A decorative effect achieved by painting a metallic pigment on the surface of a piece of porcelain or pottery and firing it in a reducing atmosphere to produce a fine metallic film. Copper, silver, gold and platinum were used to achieve different colours.
Parian ware. A fine-grained porcelain used for modelling, nearly always left in the biscuit state. First known as statuary porcelain, parian ware derived its name from its resemblance to marble from the island of Paros.
Soft paste. An imitation of hard-paste porcelain made of clay and other substances requiring a lower firing temperature than hard paste. The glaze is also fired at a lower temperature and thus appears not to 'fit' so well as the glaze on hard-paste porcelain, giving a less clear-cut impression.
Underglaze colours. Colours applied directly on to the body after the first firing. In this state the body is porous and the colour soaks in as if on blotting-paper. The piece is then glazed and given a second firing. In hard-paste porcelain, the only colours able to resist the high temperature involved are cobalt blue and copper red; these are termed *grand feu* colours.

Bibliography

Charleston, R. J., (ed) *World Ceramics*, Paul Hamlyn, London 1968
Charleston, R. J., (ed) *English Porcelain*, Ernest Benn, London 1965
Godden, G., *Victorian Porcelain*, Herbert Jenkins, London 1961
Honey, W. B., *Dresden China*, Faber and Faber, London new edition 1954
Honey, W. B., *Ceramic Art from the end of the Middle Ages to about 1815* (2 vols), Faber and Faber, London 1952
Honey, W. B., *The Ceramic Art of China and other Countries of the Far East*, Faber and Faber, London 1945
Honey, W. B., *French Porcelain of the Eighteenth Century*, Faber and Faber, London 1950
Honey, W. B., *English Pottery and Porcelain*, A. C. Black, London 1962 (revised ed)
Honey, W. B., *Old English Porcelain*, Faber and Faber, London 1948 (2nd ed)
Jenyns, S., *Japanese Porcelain*, Faber and Faber, London 1965
Lane, A., *Italian Porcelain*, Faber and Faber, London 1954
Savage, G., *Eighteenth Century German Porcelain*, Barrie and Rockcliff, London 1958
Verlet, P., Grandjean, D., and Bruent, M., *Sèvres*, Prat, Paris 1954 (2 vols)
Watney, B., *English Blue and White Porcelain of the Eighteenth Century*, Faber and Faber, London 1961

Acknowledgements
Barrie and Jenkins, London: 28, 29. B.P.C. Publishing Limited, London: 1, 2, 3, 6, 8, 9, 10, 11, 12, 18, 19, 20, 21, 22, 23, 24, 26, 30, 31, 32, 33, 34, 35, 36, 37, 38, 39, 40, 41, 42, 43, 52, 53, 59, 60, 63, 66, 67, 68, 69, 70, 71, 72, 73, 74, 75, 76, 78, 87, 88, 89, 90, 91, 92, 93, 94, 95, 101, 102, 103, 104, 105, 106, 107, 108, 109, 110. Connaissance des Arts, Paris: 16, 45, 48. Fitzwilliam Museum, Cambridge: 25, 27. J. Freeman, London: 50, 54, 55, 56, 57, 58. Geoffrey Godden: 82, 83, 84, 85, 86, 96, 97. By gracious permission of H.M. The Queen: 61. Philadelphia Museum of Art, Philadelphia: 49. George Rainbird Limited, London: 77. Réalités, Paris: 17, 46, 47, 62. Victoria and Albert Museum, London: 4, 5, 7, 13, 14, 15, 44, 64, 65, 79, 80, 81, 98, 99, 100. Wadsworth Atheneum, Connecticut: 51.

1 *Dishes*, Ming Dynasty, Chêng Tê period (1506–21). (Private Collection.) Both these dishes are decorated with the Imperial yellow glaze. That on the left is finely incised with dragons and the plain bowl on the right, of which only the base is illustrated, bears the six-character reign-mark of the Emperor Chêng Tê. Imperial yellow table services consisted of dishes and bowls only, and each piece always bore the reign-mark of the emperor for whom they were made.

1

2

3

2 Left: *Chinese dish.* Early fifteenth century. Right: *Turkish dish.* Early seventeenth century. (Private Collection.) Both recently found in Damascus, these dishes show the importance of Chinese porcelain to Near Eastern pottery design. The Turkish dish, in tin-glazed earthenware, is a faithful copy of the Chinese piece.

3 Behind: *Serving-dish of kraak porselyn*, Ming Dynasty, Wan Li period (1573–1620). (Christie, Manson and Woods, London.) These early export wares, brought in large quantities to the West by the Dutch East India Company, derived their name from the Portuguese trading ships, the Carracas. Left: *Provincial dish*, Chinese. Early sixteenth century. Probably intended for the South East Asia market, these dishes were the first mass-produced wares for everyday use. This dish is painted in the diluted blue which was used for these much cheaper types. Right: *Ginger-jar*. Ch'ing dynasty, K'ang Hsi period (1662–1722). Under K'ang Hsi much blue-and-white ware was made, painted in a reverberating cobalt and often decorated with the 'flowers of the four seasons' – prunus, peony, lotus and chrysanthemum.

4 *Plate*, K'ang Hsi period. (Victoria and Albert Museum, London.) This plate is decorated in underglaze blue with pine branches, a lady and a *ch'i-lin* (a Chinese unicorn, symbol of virtue).

5 *Vase*, K'ang Hsi period. (Victoria and Albert Museum, London.) This simple vase shows a much sought-after apple green colour. The translucent coating of emerald green is applied over a white glaze which has been deliberately crazed.

6 *Tou T'sai jar*, Ming Dynasty, Ch'êng Hua period (1468–87). (Private Collection.) Although this jar has been extensively repaired, it is an excellent example of the earliest type of enamel painting done in China. This was the last major problem to be solved in the potter's art, and the solution, using a 'muffle kiln', was discovered late in the fifteenth century.

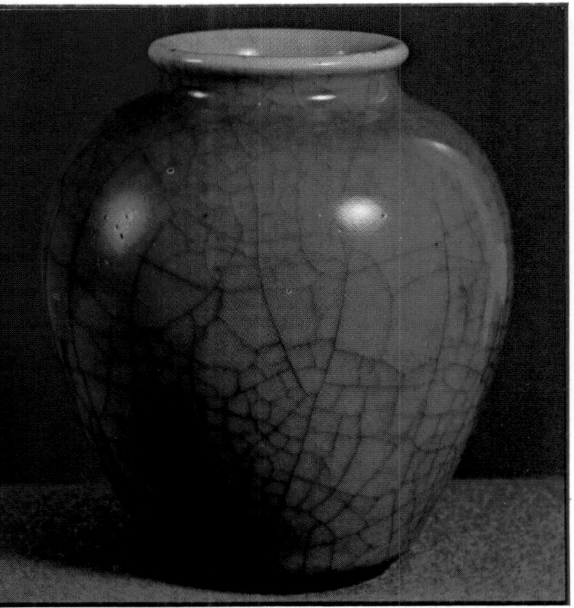

6

7

9

7 *Kettle*, Ch'ing Dynasty, Yung Chêng period (1723–35). (Victoria and Albert Museum, London.) Some of the finest monochrome glazes were introduced in the reign of Yung Chêng as well as some particularly fine reproductions of Ming wares. The handle and spout of this kettle, which is decorated with a yellow glaze, are modelled in the form of dragons.

8 *Bowl*, Chinese. Mid nineteenth century. (Private Collection.) Painted in *famille rose* enamels and decorated with panels, this bowl belongs to the large group of porcelains which bear only 'hallmarks'. These wares were intended for palace rooms, pavilions, retreats or similar places. Frequently these 'hallmarks' refer to fanciful establishments; in this instance the iron-red mark refers to 'the hall of brilliant colours'.

9 *Vase*, Ch'ing Dynasty, Hsien Fêng mark and period (1851–61). (Mrs. E. Hatoum Collection.) The decorative repertoire in the nineteenth century, apart from the delicate 'Chinese taste' flowers and birds, is often drawn from both Buddhist and Taoist mythology. This vase, painted in *famille rose* enamels, shows on the one side Shou Lao, the God of Longevity, holding some peaches, an emblem of longevity, and Liu Hai with his three-legged toad spewing cash, symbolic of wealth and good fortune.

10

10 *Small hexagonal wine-cup*, Nabeshima. Early eighteenth century. (Private Collection.) One c the notable successes of the Nabeshima pottery was the mastery of painting in underglaze blue. Th colour of the blue is soft, lending itself admirably as a base for overglaze colours which achieved high degree of excellence.

11 *Oviform vase*, Satsuma. Second half of the nineteenth century. (Christie, Manson and Woods London.) The early porcelain 'souvenir' pieces of Japan, such as this decorative vase, were of a fin quality which later often descended into extreme vulgarity.

12 *Buddhistic Lion*, Kakiemon. Second half of the seventeenth century. (Christie, Manson an Woods.) The highly decorative designs and colour schemes produced by the Japanese Kakiemo family made such an impact on the European market that all the major porcelain factories i Europe produced pieces in direct imitation. The base of this lion is painted with typical octopu scroll decoration in association with peony flowers.

11

12

13 *Cane-handle*, Saint-Cloud. *c.*1725–50. (Victoria and Albert Museum, London.) This attractive handle, in the form of a mermaid, was designed for a walking-stick and is an excellent example of the popular enamel painting used on Saint-Cloud porcelain during the first half of the eighteenth century. The style, employing bold colours, is in direct imitation of the Japanese Arita porcelain decorated in the Kakiemon manner.

16

14

15

17

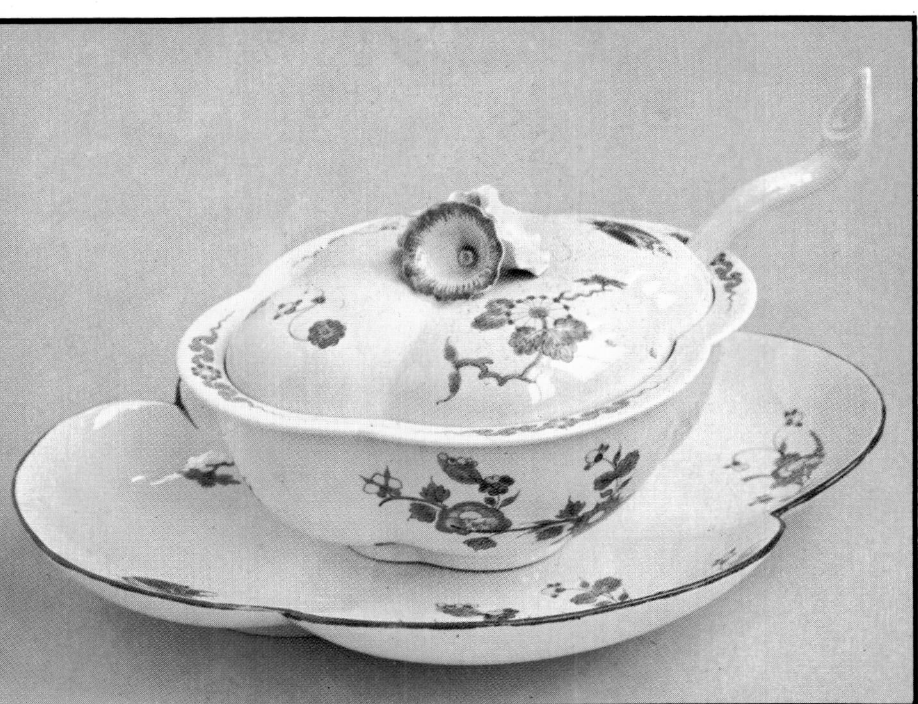

14 *Snuff-box*, Saint-Cloud. The silver mount marked in Paris, 1738–39. (Victoria and Albert Museum, London.) Silver mounts are particularly useful in dating such pieces as this charming little snuff-box moulded in the form of a hunter at rest and picked out with the typical, bold, enamel colours of Saint-Cloud wares.

15 *Teapot and cover*, Saint-Cloud. Marked with a sun-face in blue, *c.*1725. (Victoria and Albert Museum, London.) The underglaze-blue decoration is in the style made popular by Daniel Marot and is influenced also by contemporary silver design.

16 *Pot-pourri vase*, Saint-Cloud. *c.*1725–35. (Musée des Arts Décoratifs, Paris.) This large vase, decorated with the moulded flowers and scales in relief which are typical of this period, would have been used to hold dry petals and spices.

17 *Figure of a seated man*, Chantilly. Second quarter of the eighteenth century. (Musée des Arts Décoratifs, Paris.) The naturalistic flower painting on the robes of this attractive figure show the influence of Meissen *Indianische Blumen.*

18 *Sugar-bowl, stand, cover and perforated spoon*, Mennecy. Mid eighteenth century. (Victoria and Albert Museum, London.) This bowl shows a more highly developed sense of the Rococo than the Chantilly version in 19. The shell volute lid, fluted stand and naturalistic flower painting are typical of the Mennecy factory.

19 *Sugar-bowl, stand, cover and perforated spoon*, Chantilly. Second quarter of the eighteenth century. This is a typical piece from the first period of the Chantilly factory with the characteristic milky-white glaze, Kakiemon-style decoration and three-flower knop.

20 *Pair of stoppered flasks*, Meissen. *c.*1717–19. (Victoria and Albert Museum, London.) Deriving their shape from Japanese *saké* bottles, these spirit or cordial flasks pre-date the great enamel colour innovations made at Meissen in the 1720s.

21 *Cup and saucer*, Meissen. 1716–20. (Victoria and Albert Museum, London.) Böttger must take the credit for the mother of pearl lustre, which was first used with gold in 1716.

22 *Virgin of the Immaculate Conception* by J. J. Kändler (1706–75). 1737. (Victoria and Albert Museum, London.) This miniature figure illustrates how the baroque concept of sculpture was interpreted in the new medium of porcelain.

23

24

23 *Allegory of Summer* by F. E. Meyer. *c.*1752. (Victoria and Albert Museum, London.) This figure, painted with enamel colours and gold, comes from a set representing the seasons. F. E. Meyer (born 1724) joined the Meissen factory in 1748 and introduced the small heads and elongated bodies which are characteristic of mid-eighteenth-century Meissen.

24 *Shepherd with Bagpipes*, Meissen. Mid eighteenth century. (Victoria and Albert Museum, London.) The vitality of this figure suggests that Kändler was the modeller. It indicates his superiority over later and lesser artists who produced insipid pastoral figures.

27

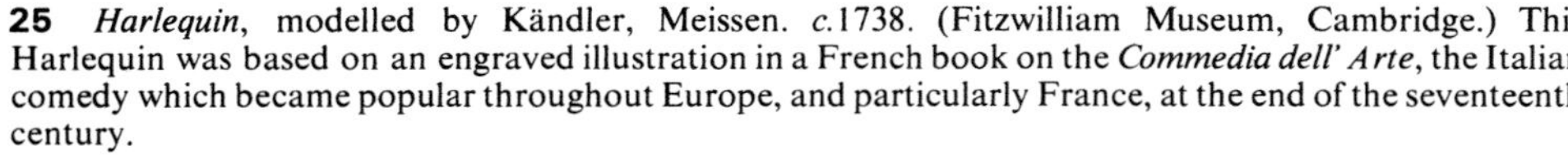

25 *Harlequin*, modelled by Kändler, Meissen. *c.*1738. (Fitzwilliam Museum, Cambridge.) This Harlequin was based on an engraved illustration in a French book on the *Commedia dell' Arte*, the Italian comedy which became popular throughout Europe, and particularly France, at the end of the seventeenth century.

26 *Plate from the Swan Service* by Kändler, Meissen. 1738. (Victoria and Albert Museum, London.) Comprising some 2,200 pieces in thirty different forms, the Swan Service is the most spectacular of all porcelain services, and takes its name from the subtle swan reliefs that appear most conspicuously on the plates.

27 *Woman carrying a child* by Kändler, Meissen. 1744. (Fitzwilliam Museum, Cambridge.) Painted with enamelled colours, Kändler has adapted a French engraving of 1739 of a peasant woman of Savoy.

25

26

28 *The Happy Parents*, Meissen. Late eighteenth century, marked with incised crossed swords in a triangle and 'E3' and '183'. (Victoria and Albert Museum, London.) In the mid nineteenth century, Meissen was producing large numbers of groups and busts in biscuit, but the material never achieved the beauty of French or English biscuit, and old moulds were brought out and used quite indiscriminately. This is a typical neoclassical group after a model by M. Acier (died 1799).

29

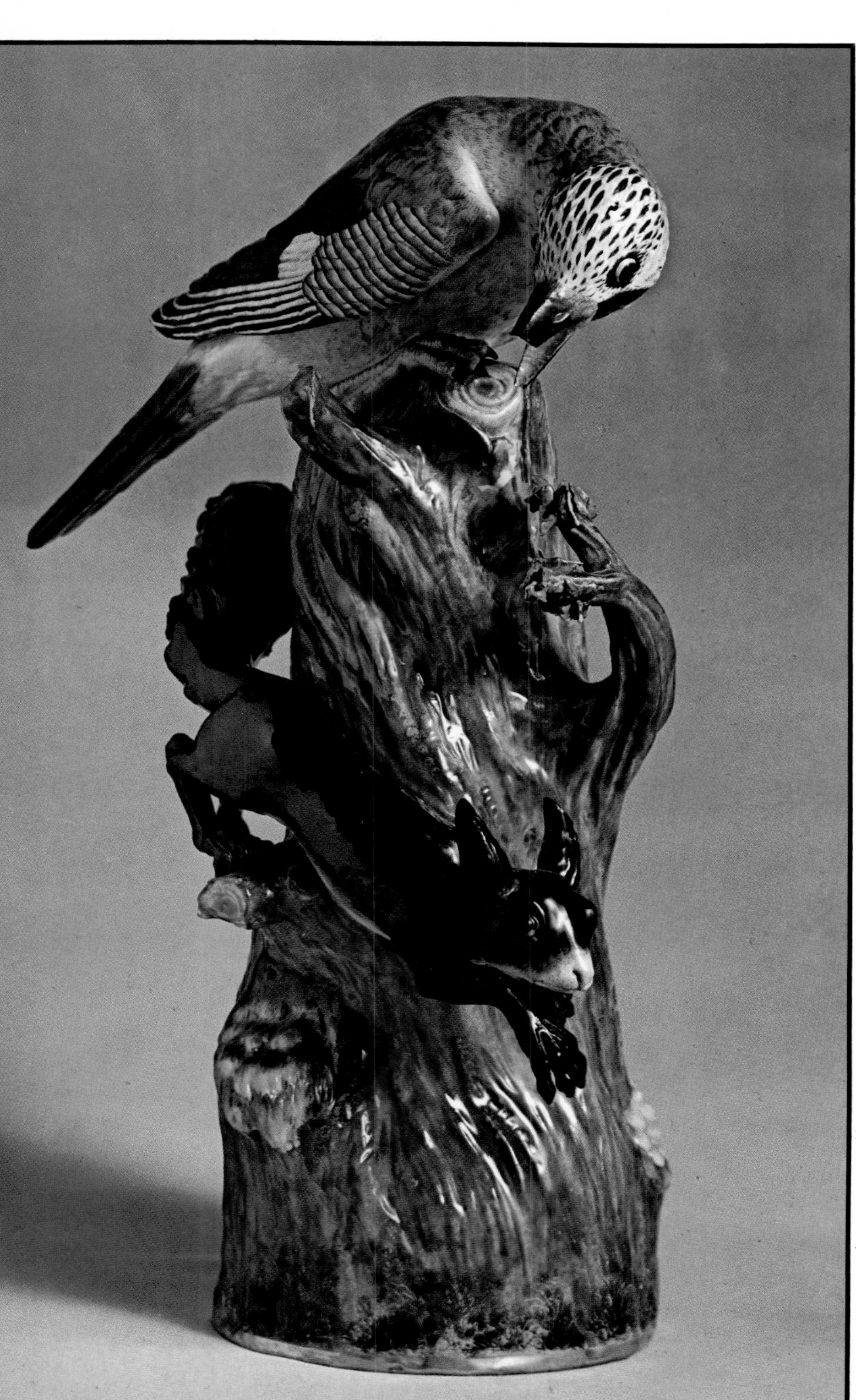

29 *Vase of flowers*, Meissen. Mid nineteenth century. (Private Collection.) The rococo model for this piece is very seldom found in its eighteenth-century form, but the nineteenth-century reproduction is quite common. Pink and turquoise combined with gilding is characteristic of Meissen porcelain of this period.

30 *Jay*, Meissen. Mid nineteenth century. (Private Collection.) This is a version of Kändler's figure of a jay of 1739–40, though the surface is shinier and the decoration bolder and, in the original, more of the porcelain was left unpainted. A number of old moulds were re-used during this period and, indeed, so much of the Meissen output was reproduction that in 1846 the Minister of Finance pronounced that a new and 'pure and noble style' should be sought after.

31

32

33

37

31 *Teapot*, Nymphenburg. Mid eighteenth century. (Victoria and Albert Museum, London.) Of the many other porcelain works set up to rival Meissen, Nymphenburg produced some of the most beautiful and distinguished wares in the German rococo style. The naturalistic flowers employed on this teapot were one of their favourite decorative devices.

32 *Stand for a food-warmer*, Nymphenburg. Mid eighteenth century. (Victoria and Albert Museum, London.) Among the wide range of tablewares made at Nymphenburg during the eighteenth century, food-warmers were a new addition, consisting of a small, hollow pedestal in which rested a covered bowl with a projecting flange. The naturalistic decoration is combined with delightful asymmetrical scrolls.

33 *Tureen and cover*, Vienna. *c.*1735. (Victoria and Albert Museum, London.) Many sumptuous pieces such as this tureen were made as gifts for the Russian court. The applied masks indicate that silver shapes and designs were relied upon in the absence of a tradition of porcelain forms.

34 *Wine-cooler*, Vienna. *c.*1740. (Victoria and Albert Museum, London.) Using many of the Meissen techniques, and even some of their craftsmen, the Vienna porcelain factory produced individual and intricate wares in hard-paste. This wine-cooler is decorated in polychrome with flowers and a mouse.

35 *Tea-caddy*, Vienna. *c.*1725–30. (Victoria and Albert Museum, London.) Painted with *chinoiseries* in the manner of the engraved designs of Elias Baeck, the iron red of the baroque palette is muted, foreshadowing the later subtleties of the rococo.

36 *Tureen*, Vienna. *c.*1725–35. (Victoria and Albert Museum, London.) Decorated in brownish *schwarzlot* heightened with gilding, this unusually large tureen is decorated with hunting scenes as well as the more usual baroque designs of Viennese porcelain.

37 *Bottle*, Vienna. *c.*1725–35. (Österreichisches Museum, Vienna.) In best baroque fashion, this handsome bottle is topped by a bust of a Roman emperor. Decorated in *schwarzlot* and heightened with gilding, the piece combines Austrian and Japanese elements.

38
39
40
41

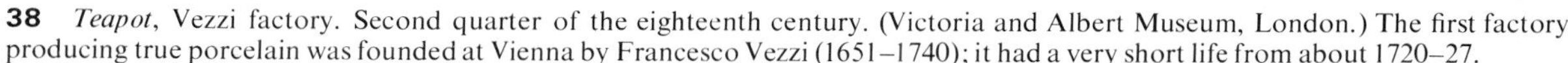

38 *Teapot*, Vezzi factory. Second quarter of the eighteenth century. (Victoria and Albert Museum, London.) The first factory producing true porcelain was founded at Vienna by Francesco Vezzi (1651–1740); it had a very short life from about 1720–27.

39 *Plate*, signed by Cozzi, the founder of the third Venetian porcelain factory. 1780. (Victoria and Albert Museum, London.) Decorated in the style of Sèvres, this plate is painted with the story of Europa and the Bull, after a painting by Paolo Veronese. The reserve panels around the border contain miniatures of the Tiepolo and Tintoretto masterpieces in the Doges' Palace in Venice.

40 *Teacup and saucer*, Cozzi factory. Late eighteenth century. (Victoria and Albert Museum, London.) These fine pieces are decorated in polychrome with a Venetian *Capriccio*.

41 *Tea-caddy*, Vezzi factory. Second quarter of the eighteenth century. (Victoria and Albert Museum, London.) Painted in polychrome with a pseudo-oriental design, this attractive caddy is similar to contemporary metalwork, and indicates Vezzi's early training as a goldsmith.

42 *Saucer*, Hewelcke factory, 1761–63. (Victoria and Albert Museum, London.) Founded by N. F. Hewelcke and his wife, who had emigrated to Venice from Dresden, this factory produced wares of inferior quality to those of Vezzi and Cozzi. The shapes are comparatively clumsy and the glazes and colours lack brilliance.

42

43

44

43 *Pisces*, Buen Retiro. *c.*1775–80. (Victoria and Albert Museum, London.) When Charles III, King of the Two Sicilies, succeeded to the throne of Spain, reluctant to leave behind the porcelain factory he had founded at Capodimonte, he set up a similar factory at Buen Retiro. The early pieces are difficult to distinguish from Capodimonte, as most of them were made from paste imported from Italy. This figure, from a series of the signs of the zodiac, is made from a fine creamy paste and is marked with a *fleur-de-lis*.

44 *Holy water stoup*, Buen Retiro. *c.*1780. (Victoria and Albert Museum, London.) The later utilitarian output of the Buen Retiro factory is in soft paste and much whiter than the earlier ware. The mark from 1760–1804 was the Bourbon *fleur-de-lis*, in blue or gold, sometimes used with the initials of the workmen. This holy water stoup is painted and gilt.

45 *Vase*, Capodimonte, painted by Maria Caselli. 1750. (Victoria and Albert Museum, London.) Vases of this type were frequently made at the Capodimonte factory. The design is based on Meissen Augustus Rex vases made for the porcelain enthusiast Augustus the Strong, Elector of Saxony.

45

46 *Plate*, Vincennes. *c.*1750. (Musée National de Céramique, Sèvres.) Birthplace of the famous Sèvres factory, the royal workshops at Vincennes, encouraged by Louis XV, produced distinctive and beautiful wares in soft-paste porcelain. This plate, painted with vignettes of a cupid and vines *en camaïeu*, is an example of the simpler wares for everyday use which were produced at Vincennes.

47 *Plate*, Vincennes. Mid eighteenth century. (Louvre, Paris.) Magnificent serving-dishes probably formed a part of the many sets of tableware which provided the basic reserve for the Vincennes factory. These were frequently painted with flower designs in an asymmetrical rococo setting, as on this example. Gilding was used copiously for the first time in France at Vincennes, and the effect was particularly interesting when the gilding was used for engraving, as illustrated here by the flowers.

49

48

50

48 *Girl with a bird-cage*, Vincennes. Dated 1753. (Musée National de Céramique, Sèvres.) Crying over the loss of her bird, this charming girl was inspired by a picture by Boucher, which was adapted by Blondeau in 1752.

49 *Cup and saucer*, Vincennes. Mid eighteenth century. (Musée des Arts Décoratifs, Paris.) Cupids floating on clouds were a favourite motif for the central panels of plates. In this case, the theme has been given a most luxurious treatment with a rich border of cobalt blue and heavy gilding around the pink cupid painted *en camaïeu*.

50 *Vase*, one of a pair, Vincennes. *c.*1755. (Philadelphia Museum of Art. Bequest of Eleanor Elkins Rice.) By 1753, a growing partiality for coloured grounds in the manner of Meissen had become apparent at the Vincennes factory. Panels of varying shape or, as in this instance, a cartouche, were reserved in white against these grounds, and within them were created marvellous miniature paintings.

Pot-pourri, Sèvres. *c.*1755–60. (Wallace Collection, London.) Table centres in a design vaguely suggesting a rigged ship, known as a *vaisseau à mât* (ship with a mast), e splendid examples of early Sèvres. These are in three parts: a stand with four scrolled legs; a boat-shaped rose-water vessel, the top pierced with circular holes to allow e scent to perfume the room, and the lid, which is shaped as a central mast supporting formalized sails and rigging.

Fountain, Vincennes. Mid eighteenth century. (Wadsworth Athenaeum, Hartford, Connecticut. J. P. Morgan Collection.) Large fountains of this sort, also made in ver, were used to serve wine or other drinks on special occasions. The gilt border to the central scene on this beautiful example is akin to the gilt-bronze mounts on ntemporary furniture.

52

53

53 *Woman bathing*, copied from his own marble, exhibited in 1757, by Etienne-Maurice Falconet (1716–91), Sèvres. 1758. (Private Collection.) Director of the sculpture department at Sèvres for nine years, Falconet modelled many of the most famous biscuit figures and groups produced by the factory. This figure is the first for which Falconet used Mlle. Mistouflet as a model; she is seen later in various other works. Falconet's work has a character which differentiates it from earlier and later biscuit. He always strove for liveliness and realism and while the figures themselves are no less conventional than those of other periods they do suggest movement whereas the others record a figure in a moment of time. Falconet's natural aesthetic tendency and early training are the key to this difference; he showed himself for what he was, a baroque artist working in a rococo milieu.

54 *The Kiss*, by Falconet, Sèvres. 1765. (Private Collection.) Like many figures and groups modelled by Falconet, this charming pair is based on a design by the artist François Boucher. An advantage in collecting Sèvres soft-paste biscuit is that, unlike decorated Sèvres, there are no fakes.

55

55 *Toilet-service*, Sèvres. Bearing date-letters 'K' and 'L' for 1763–64. (Wallace Collection, London.) Toilet-sets made of Sèvres porcelain, of which this is a part, are rarely found. It is probable that few were made and many were broken. This set, painted by Parpette, is said to have been used by Louis XVI.

56 *Teapot*, Sèvres. Bearing date-letter 'Q' for 1769. (Wallace Collection, London.) Decorated by the painter J. Fontaine with blue *œil de perdrix*, a characteristic Sèvres device consisting of tiny circles or double circles of dots, often found in sea green or bright blue, in which reserves are set against the monochrome or dotted ground. In this instance, the reserves are decorated with profile heads in monochrome and are surrounded by cameo wreaths and ribbons.

57 *Saucer*, Sèvres. Bearing date-letter 'H' for 1760. (Wallace Collection, London.) This piece is painted by Vieillard, whose characteristic style, like that of another Sèvres painter, Dodin, is distinguished by its bias towards gay and amorous subjects and children's games.

58 *Breakfast-service*, Sèvres. Bearing date-letter 'L' for 1761. (Wallace Collection, London.) This breakfast-service, consisting of a tray, sugar-basin and cup and saucer, is decorated in the popular rose marbled with gold and blue. It was the enameller Xhrouet who invented the *rose carné* ground-colour in 1757 which was a pure opaque flesh-tint, difficult to achieve; if the firing temperature was too high, it was converted to a dirty yellow; if too low, it became brownish and mottled.

56

7

59

60

9 *Cup and saucer*, Sèvres. 1776. (Wallace Collection, London.) Made in hard paste, the rich *bleu de roi*, a dark blue, seen on this magnificent cup and saucer, was one f the most popular of the new enamel ground-colours. The reserve panels, showing trophies and scenes of children at play, were probably painted by J. Fontaine (active 752–1801).

0 *Cream-jug and cup and saucer*, Sèvres. 1775 and 1769. (Victoria and Albert Museum, London.) The deep green ground of the cream-jug provides an ideal foil for the mantic paintings in the style of Boucher by Noël. The cup and saucer were probably painted by Asselin and are in the typical rococo style.

1 *Pair of candlesticks*, Sèvres. 1775–85. (Victoria and Albert Museum, London.) Made of hard-paste porcelain mounted in ormolu, these candlesticks mark the transition om the light fantasy of the rococo style to the more grandiloquent and serious style which succeeded it.

62 *Detail of a classical medallion*, Sèvres. (Musée National de Céramique, Sèvres.) Sèvres porcelain was used for diplomatic gifts, as we know from the 'register' of the king's presents in the archives of the Ministry of Foreign Affairs, and from the accounts of the factory itself, in which are noted numerous deliveries of large dinner-services to foreign sovereigns. This detail is from a part of the dinner-service made for the Empress Catherine II of Russia.

63 *Vase*, Sèvres. *c.*1768. (By gracious permission of H.M. the Queen.) Made of soft-paste porcelain with an apple-green ground and a fir-cone knop, this vase is of a shape known as *vase à filet ruban.* In the reserved panel painted by, or in the manner of, Morin is a camp scene, while a military trophy is depicted on the back. Decorative vases such as this were made in both hard- and soft-paste porcelain, and were one of the most important products of Sèvres at this date.

62

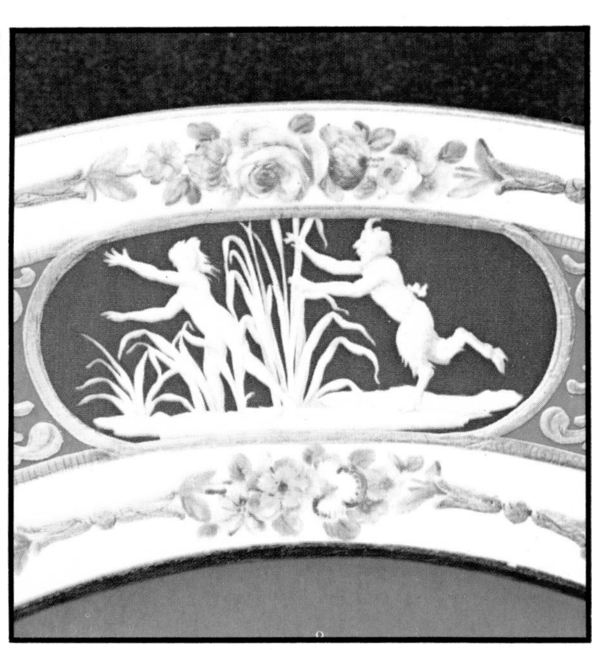

63

64 *Veilleuse* (tea-warmer), rue Faubourg Saint-Denis, Paris. 1803–35, marked 'Flassen Fleury à Paris' stencilled in red. (Victoria and Albert Museum, London.) The upper half of this piece forms a teapot with spout, lid and handle, while the base serves as a supporting pedestal to house the small oil-lamp.

65 *Jug*, French, probably Paris. *c.*1825–30. (Victoria and Albert Museum, London.) This jug could well be taken as a typical example of 'Rockingham-type' revived Rococo, but it is in fact French hard-paste porcelain. It bears no factory mark, but has incised workers' marks on the base under the glaze, a feature often seen on the hard-paste porcelains of other continental manufactories.

66

66 *Two figures*, Samson. (Samson Manufacture de Porcelaines, Faïences et Terres Cuites, Montreuil sous-Bois, near Paris.) T tradition of imitation and even of blatant plagiarism is firmly rooted in the history of ceramics. Generally, however, it is just o aspect of the production of a factory, which otherwise produces original wares. To this rule, the Samson factory in Paris provid the outstanding exception, for, at least until recently, this factory devoted itself entirely to the meticulous imitation of other a earlier factories, although the precise attribution of this group cannot be identified.

67 *Tartar archer*, after J. Kändler and P. Reinicke of the Meissen factory in Germany, Popov Factory, Moscow. *c.*18 (Dashwood Collection, West Wycombe Park, Buckinghamshire.) Just before 1800, there were a number of private porcela factories functioning in Russia. Apart from the most famous, the Kievo-Mezhigorskaya Fabrika at Kiev, there was the porcela manufactory started at the village of Gorbunov, near Moscow, by Carl Melli in 1806, which was bought in 1811 by the Mosc merchant A. G. Popov and continued in operation until the mid nineteenth century. The best products of this factory appear between 1811 and the year of Popov's death in 1850.

68 *Plate*, by F. Y. Gardner. 1780. (Sotheby and Co., London.) Early Gardner porcelain does not compare with the cool whi ness of Meissen nor with the purity of the St. Petersburg factory, but it does show a lovely off-white hue more reminiscent Chinese export products. Catherine II extended her patronage and commissioned Gardner to make grand services decorated w ribbons, badges and stars of the leading Imperial orders of chivalry for use on the annual gala occasions held in the Winter Pala in honour of the Knights of the Order. The St. Alexander Nevsky Service, commissioned in 1777, of which this plate is a part, i triumph of the decorator's art, the rich crimson of the moiré ribbon being particularly spectacular.

69 *Plate*, Imperial Porcelain Factory, St. Petersburg. 1814–17. (Palace of Pavlovsk, near Leningrad.) A famous set of porcel still surviving, of which this plate forms a part, is the Gur'yevsky Service, named after and commissioned by Count Gur'y President of the Cabinet in 1809. The service was designed mainly by S. S. Pimenov in the Empire style. The colours are de Etruscan red and gold, painted with views of St. Petersburg, military and genre scenes and vignettes taken from the work of English artist D. A. Atkinson (1775–1831).

68

69

70

71

70 *Farmyard clock-case*, Chelsea. Marked with a red anchor. *c.*1755. (Private Collection.) The Chelsea factory, possibly the earliest English factory, produced fine and beautifully decorated wares, largely inspired by Meissen and the Orient. The figures of the red anchor period were the glory of Chelsea porcelain. The modelling and skilful attention to detail reached a standard never surpassed in English wares. This delightful example still holds its original clock.

71 *Plates*, Chelsea. *c.*1750–52 and *c.*1752–54. (Private Collection.) The decoration on these plates is in imitation of the Kakiemon style; there are spur-marks on the bases where the pieces rested during firing.

72

73

72 *La Nourrice*, also called *The Chellsea Nurs*, Chelsea. Marked with a red anchor. *c.*1755. (Victoria a Albert Museum, London.) In the phase from roughly 1752–58, when the factory mark was a red anch the modeller Joseph Willems created a 'factory style'. Although many of his models were direct copi from Meissen, others were adapted from engravings or, as in this instance, a sixteenth-century piece ma near Fontainebleau.

73 *Octagonal bowl and saucer*, Chelsea. Red anchor period. *c.*1755. (Private Collection.) The pieces were possibly painted by the original fable painter J. H. O'Neale, who painted many anim subjects for Worcester at a later date but never surpassed his early work at Chelsea.

Scent-bottle, Chelsea. Gold anchor period. *c.*1760. (Private Collection.) Scent-bottles continued delight in London as elsewhere, and these and other small objects, such as needle-cases, *bonbonnières* d seals were exported freely to the Continent.

Goat and bee jug, Chelsea. Marked with an incised triangle, *c.*1745. (Cecil Higgins Art Gallery, dford, by permission of the Trustees.) Early Chelsea porcelain was of a very attractive quality, hly translucent and based on glass ingredients. A number of pieces which were produced in this t period, the 'triangle' period, bear close affinities to Sprimont's silverwork. These pieces appear some of his porcelain wares, although the curious cream-jugs, the bottom part of which were ulded in the form of a goat and which usually have a bee above the goat's head, derive from the rk of other silversmiths.

Madonna and Child, Chelsea. Red anchor period, *c.*1755. (Cecil Higgins Art Gallery, Bedford, permission of the Trustees.) The figures of the red anchor period are perhaps the chief glory of glish porcelain, although many of them derive from the work of Kändler and Reinicke at Meissen. in this example, the Chelsea adaptations were probably created mainly by Joseph Willems from ussels who stayed with the factory for most of its independent existence. The probable source for s design was a painting by Van Dyck.

75

76

The Music Lesson, Chelsea. Gold anchor period, *c.*1765. (Victoria and Albert Museum, London.) This delightful scene is based on a painting by the French artist ançois Boucher (1703–70), called '*L'agréable Leçon*'.

Musician, Bow. Painted with a large 'A' in underglaze blue and an anchor and dagger painted in red enamel. *c.*1765. (Victoria and Albert Museum, London.) Bow, ›ugh not of such high quality as Chelsea porcelain, was both stronger and cheaper to produce and could therefore compete more successfully with Oriental wares.

79

79 *Plate*, Bow. *c.*1770. (Victoria and Albert Museum, London.) Bow endeavoured to compete with the extravagant wares made at Chelsea during the gold anchor period (*c.*1758–70). This plate illustrates an attempt to imitate both the 'Mazarin' blue and the exotic birds of Chelsea.

80 *Teapot*, Bow. *c.*1753. (Victoria and Albert Museum, London.) This blue-and-white teapot is a fine example of early Bow. It has the typical translucency of the well-fired body showing a pale greenish to straw-coloured hue by artificial light. The pattern shows the well-known banana tree, fence and bird, on a distinctive globular shaped pot with a similarly shaped knop.

80

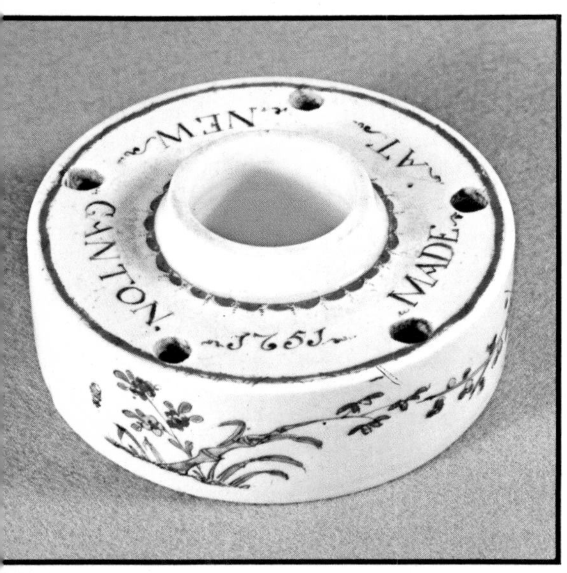

81 *Inkwell*, Bow. 1751. (Victoria and Albert Museum, London.) Painted in enamelled colours and one of the earliest dated pieces of Bow, this inkwell is inscribed 'Made at New Canton 1751'.

82 *Teapot*, Lowestoft. *c.*1785. (Private Collection.) Situated on the Suffolk coast, the fishing town of Lowestoft produced some exceptional pieces of porcelain although its international fame was based on an error by nineteenth-century ceramic writers, who attributed to this factory a class of Chinese porcelain made expressly for the European and American market.

83 *'Trifle' mug*, Lowestoft. *c.*1790. (L. Godden Collection.) 'Trifles' were sold as part of the tourist trade at most fashionab watering places in the eighteenth-century.

84 *Flask*, Lowestoft. *c.*1780. (Private Collection.) A fine example of underglaze blue painting showing a man-of-war being bu on a local beach.

85 *Tea-caddy*, Lowestoft. 1797. (Private Collection.) Decorated in the style of some of the birth discs, this tea-caddy commemorat the birth of the marriage of a local girl.

86 *Coffee-pot*, Lowestoft. *c.*1775. (Mr. and Mrs. Hutchinson Collection.) Decorated in overglaze enamels in conjunction wi underglaze blue, this coffee-pot is in the style known as 'Redgrave', after a family of painters of this name who were employed the factory and are believed to have specialized in these designs.

83

85

84

86

90

89

91

7 *Sauce-boat*, Derby. *c.*1765. (Private Collection.) Derby can rightly claim, with Chelsea, Bow and Worcester, to be one of the most distinguished eighteenth-century nglish porcelain factories. Decorated in underglaze blue with an oriental brocade pattern on the outside and a river scene inside.

8 *Figure of a negro boy*, Derby. *c.*1765. (Victoria and Albert Museum, London.) This figure could have been intended either for sweetmeats or purely as an ornament.

9 *Covered pot*, Derby. *c.*1760. (Victoria and Albert Museum, London.) Exquisitely painted with scenes of the English countryside and with delicate insects, this small ot is finished with an unusual Pan's head.

0 *Bowl with cover and stand*, Derby. *c.*1775. (Victoria and Albert Museum, London.)

1 *Figure of Britannia*, Derby. *c.*1765. (Victoria and Albert Museum, London.) It is probable that more figures were made by the Derby factory than by any other English actory. Practical wares prior to 1770 are rarer.

92

92 *Vases and Covers*, Worcester. Early Dr. Wall period, *c.*1755–58. (Dyson Perrins Museum, Royal Porcelain Works, Worcester.) The superiority of early Worcester porcelain lay largely in its quality of heat resistance. These vases are decorated with overglaze paintings of flower and bird subjects in the Meissen style.

93 Left: *Teapot*, with turquoise (*blue céleste*) ground, Worcester. *c.*1775. Right: *Coffee-pot* with reserved panels on a yellow ground, Worcester. *c.*1765. *Sugar-bowl and cover*, with reserved panels on a green ground, Worcester. *c.*1770. *Coffee-cup and saucer*, with painting by the 'Cut Fruit painter' on reserved panels in a claret ground, Worcester. *c.*1770. (Dyson Perrins Museum, Royal Porcelain Works, Worcester.)

93

95

94 *Tankard*, Worcester, *c.*1754. (Private Collection.) Worcester tankards were produced in a wide variety of shapes and sizes, the design and decoration of all showing an attractive blend of care and vigour. Nearly all the Worcester wares of this period show a beautiful green translucency when held up to direct light.

95 *Vase and cover*, Worcester, *c.*1760. (Dyson Perrins Museum, Royal Porcelain Works, Worcester.) Their overglaze painting covers a very wide range from flowers and birds in the Meissen style of the early to mid 1750s; the Chinese, as illustrated here, and Japanese styles of the late '50s to '60s; to the sophisticated London styles of the late '60s to '70s. These are broadly the dates of the general introduction of the styles at Worcester although the periods of course tended to overlap.

96

97

96 *Teapot*, Caughley, decorated outside the factory, probably by Chamberlain at Worcester, *c.*1785–90. (Private Collection.) Records exist of thousands of objects which were made at the Caughley factory and shipped down the river Severn to be decorated by Robert Chamberlain and his enamellers and gilders at Worcester. Some pieces were then shipped back to Caughley, while others were sold by Chamberlain in his retail shop in Worcester.

97 *Presentation jug*, Caughley, inscribed 'R. Wright 1780'. (Private Collection.) Although a similar bird print is also found on Worcester wares, this blue and white jug is far superior in quality to many of the wares made at the Worcester factory in the same period.

98 *Teapot*, Longton Hall, *c.*1755. (Victoria and Albert Museum, London.) This teapot, decorated with enamelled colours and a bunch of grapes as a knop, is very typical of the Staffordshire potters' approach to porcelain – no-one but a potter conversant with a Whieldon-type earthenware would wrap a spout in a lettuce leaf. The rather ill-fitting modelling does little to help the appreciation of fine and detailed painting attributed to John Hayfield, more commonly referred to as the 'Castle Painter'. According to factory documents, Hayfield was the only painter employed at the factory for a certain period in 1755.

99 *Two putti with a goat*, Longton Hall. *c.*1755. (Victoria and Albert Museum, London.) This group, decorated in enamelled colours, is symbolic of autumn. A similar version, in which the goat is being fed with flowers, probably represents spring. This figure is one of several made from moulds which appear to have been purchased by Cookworthy, for there is little doubt that both the moulds of this group and several others were used at his Plymouth factory from 1768 for making almost identical models, although in some instances the later date calls for more fashionable bases and the addition of the background of bocage.

100 *Cupid riding a horse*, Longton Hall, *c.*1755. (Victoria and Albert Museum, London.) The Longton Hall factory often based its figure models on sculptural sources. This statuette, decorated in enamelled colours, is based on a seventeenth-century bronze by Francesco Fanelli, who is thought to have trained under the great mannerist sculptor Giovanni Bologna.

61

100

101

102

103

104

101 *Teapot*, Bristol. *c.*1755. (Private Collection.) Bristol was the home of two separate porcelain manufactories during the eighteenth century. The earlier, Lund's, made soft-paste ware from about 1748 to 1752, when it was transferred to Worcester. The later factory, which was also relatively short-lived, moved from Plymouth to Bristol in 1770. It made hard-paste porcelain until 1778 and finally closed down in 1781, before the formula was acquired for New Hall in Staffordshire.

102 *Teapot*, New Hall. Marked with the pattern number '171' and made between 1805 and 1814. (Brown Collection.) One of the most celebrated and recognizable of the New Hall forms, is this 'silver-shape' teapot. It has been given this name because it was clearly modelled after a particular form of silver teapot which would have been made first between 1770 and 1780, when neoclassical modes were straightening out rococo curves.

103 *Coffee-pot*, New Hall. *c.*1820. (Victoria and Albert Museum, London.) It is thought that stands were originally made to match these coffee-pots.

104 *Plate*, Swansea. Early nineteenth century. (National Museum of Wales, Cardiff.) Even for the grandest table-services, Swansea porcelain used the simplest shapes, often, as here, with no moulded decoration at all. The delicate painting is by William Billingsley who not only organized the painting at Swansea, but also did a certain amount himself. The flowers on this fine plate are painted with a freedom of brushwork which those of the other Swansea painters lack.

105 *Ice-pail*, Nantgarw. Early nineteenth century. (National Museum of Wales, Cardiff.) Made for the Mackintosh of Mackintosh, the service including this painted and gilt porcelain pail is an example of London decoration at its most lavish. Each piece was decorated with a different species of exotic bird in the manner of Sèvres porcelain.

106 *Plate*, New Hall. *c.*1815. (Victoria and Albert Museum, London.) This plate is decorated with purple bat-printing washed over in enamel colours. In the central reserve is fruit in a gilt basket.

107 *Plate*, New Hall. *c.*1815. (Victoria and Albert Museum, London.) This plate is also decorated with purple bat-printing washed over in enamelled colours.

106

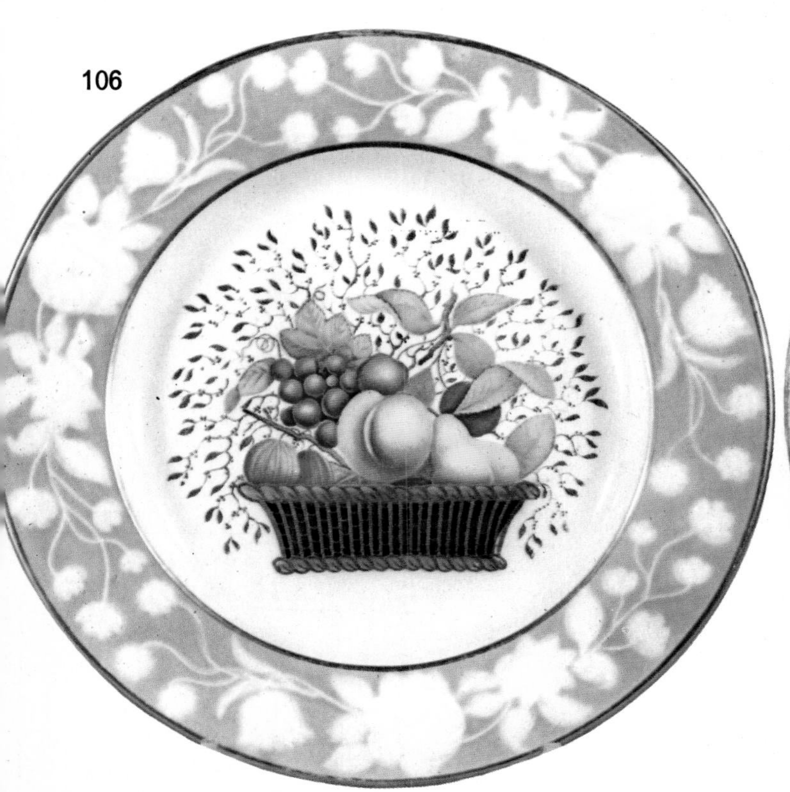

107

108

109

110

108 *Vase*, Minton. 1854. (Victoria and Albert Museum, London.) Originally created to imitate the costly and highly prized marble quarried on the Greek island of Paros, parian ware came to be used for many domestic wares and figures. This vase is decorated with passion flowers and foliage in relief, which were hand-applied to the body before firing.

109 *Clorinda and Dorothea*, Minton. 1865. (Victoria and Albert Museum, London.) Modelled by John Bell for Summerly's Art Manufacturers which were made by Minton from 1848, these parian porcelain figures were designed specifically for the South Kensington Museum, now the Victoria and Albert Museum.

110 *Vase*, Minton. *c.*1855. (Victoria and Albert Museum, London.) This vase made of enamelled bone china is combined with lightly gilt parian porcelain figures modelled by Carrier-Belleuse (1824–87).

14952

NK
4370
.C87

14952
NK 4370 .C87

CUSHION J

PORCELAIN

WITHDRAWN

Sandburg College
Learning Resource Center
Galesburg, Ill. 61401